One Vision

by Barry Auchettl

Published by Legacy Press Books
A subsidiary of S & P Productions, Inc.
311 Main Street, Suite D
El Segundo, CA 90245
310-640-8885
www.legacypressbooks.com

Text Copyright© 2020 Barry Auchettl

Cover Photography Copyright© 2020 Vincent McMahon

All rights reserved. No part of this book may be repro-duced or transmitted in any form by any means, electronic or mechanical, including photocopying, recording or by any infor-mation storage and retrieval system, without the written permis-sion of the author or publisher, except for the inclusion of brief quotations.

Published and Printed in the United States of America

ISBN: 978-1-950326-67-9

The content contained in One Vision is for informational pur-poses only. The content is not intended to be a substitute for med-ical or psychological advice, diagnosis or treatment. Always seek the advice of your physician or other qualified healthcare pro-vider with any questions you may have regarding a medical or mental health condition. Always seek the advice of qualified pro-fessionals in matters relating to any business undertakings.

Dedicated to my grandchildren Abi, Chloe, Mia and the ones yet to come, who bring so much love and joy into my life. You are indeed the next generation of change in the world.

Acknowledgements

Thank you for the people who have supported me on this journey to enable these words to get out to the world.

In particular to Adrian Hanks, David Webby, Robert Grimes, Maree Thomas, Sarah Neil, Craig Leith and Tracy Edmeades who have become family to me in Queensland.

I would also like to thank Suzi Prudden from Legacy Press for publishing this book as well as Catherine Palin-Brinkworth, Jackie McGrath and Susan Kelly who have all helped with the editing of my words.

I am honoured to have you all in my life.

Introduction

Thank you for picking up my book. It is written in appreciation for all that was given to me: the miracles of my life and my vision for a better future. I wrote it because I believe there are lessons here that will help you appreciate your life. I've had some extraordinary experiences and I really shouldn't be here and living a life that has never been better. I had a brain tumor and went missing for a while.

I went on a spiritual path and ended up where I began, but this time it was better. I want to tell you how I did it and, in the telling, inspire you to find your own light and enjoy the journey.

This is a novel of hope and light. On the surface it's the story of Joshua, who lives an ordinary life and whose life is transformed not just by his experiences but because he was willing to open his eyes to possibilities. His journey may help others be more than they are...or accept who they are by gaining a new perspective.

I want to thank the gifts and loves of my life, my former wife Jane and our children, Philip, Stephen and Carla, for taking this journey with me.

My story occurred some time ago, but the story is universal and timeless, and I hope it will inspire you to take a journey yourself and live your true selves. I would love to hear from you if you wish to share your learnings and successes with me.

In Love and Light,

Barry

More from Barry Auchettl

Workshops to See, Clear and Connect

Eye Power changes the way people see and explores all aspects of vision from physical eye exercises to intuitive vision. It is designed to increase awareness and help discover unseen potential within you. In the process, you improve your physical eyesight and your inner Vision. Barry offers workshops on **Eye Power**, **Open Your Eyes**, and **Renewed Vision** for the Workplace. For a free video on how to improve your eyesight, visit www.BarryAuchettl.com

An amazing workshop that shows you how to locate and clear sabotage programs from the subconscious mind to bring about change in all areas of your life. This frees you to enhance your goals and choose how you want your life to be. Includes **Light Body Alignments** that is a special technique Barry developed that allows blocks to be cleared in less than a minute. Barry also teaches **Insight into Muscles Testing** and **Money and The Scan Charts**.

Relationships give us the most rewarding, uplifting, exhilarating and sometimes challenging experiences in our lives. Conversations is an extraordinary board game that allows you to speak openly, be really heard and enables a genuine connection with others. Workshops include **Conversations for the Soul** which is a Conversations game experiential, **Conversations for Couples** and **Conversations for the Workplace**. Visit www.conversationsthegame.com.au

Books and Games that Uplift Humanity

Eye Power: Power your eyesight, empower your Vision. A 10 minute-a-day for 10 days guide to better vision. A little book that can make a big difference to your eyes. Other book titles include **In One Vision**, **Open Your Eyes**, **The Scan Charts** and **Conversations and Relating from the heart**. To purchase barry's books, visit www.BarryAuchettl.com or Amazon Kindle.

Conversations: an inspirational game is interactive and cooperative board game that helps develop and enhance real relationships. Neale Donald Walsch, author of Conversations with God, call it *"a fun and exciting game that will reveal the power of your God-given imagination."* Accredited Facilitation training is also available. Visit www.conversationsthegame.com.au

Mentoring and Speaking Opportunities to Inspire

Barry offers mentoring programs called **Life Vision Mentoring** which is a six month program to develop, expand and transform your Vision on all levels. He also offers speaking programs including **Creating Authentic Conversations**, **Living the Dream**, **Regaining your Natural Vision**, **Inspired Vision**, **Sabotage clearing**, and **Living the Law of Attraction**. For more details on all of Barry's programs, visit www.BarryAuchettl.com

Table of Contents

Chapter 1: New beginning 1
   The diagnosis

Chapter 2: Awakening 25
   The operation was successful. What next?

Chapter 3: Doorways 49
   Which way is the right way?

Chapter 4: A Different Way of Seeing 73
   What is reality? Who's in charge?

Chapter 5: A Different Way of Doing 97
   The spirit in healing. The process and the guides.

Chapter 6: In Dreams 121
   Dreams explored.

Chapter 7: Inner Reflections 143
   Leaving darkness and seeing the light.

Chapter 8: Universal Laws 165
   The laws of the universe. There are no coincidences.

Chapter 9: A Matter of Timing 189
   Appreciating the physical reality.

Chapter 10: Choice 211
   The road to enlightenment and a clear vision.

Chapter 11: The Journey 233
   Lost and found. Love and grace.

Chapter 12: Expectancy 257
   A vision of the future.

New Beginning

It was a crisp, frosty morning, as the sun was peeking through the clouds. Sara and I were strolling through the town. The shop windows were breaming with objects that, on a normal day we would be stopping to look at and enjoy. But not today. Today my mind was clouded with the news I had received two weeks ago.

The shops in Ballarat had been restored to their original condition from the goldfield days of the 1860s. Verandahs with carved pillars had returned to the streets over the past ten years to bring the city in line with the new heritage guidelines. Shop windows had flyers and notices about the Sovereign Hill Township, that reenacted life in the historic gold mines and battles of the days of Australia's colonisation.

As we walked by The Silver Tree, a New Age bookshop, I stopped to look at the displays of ceramic

One Vision

wizards and dragons that occupied most of the window. My eyes fell upon a purple paper stuck to the window with a handwritten scrawl, Meditation, 10:30 am, Tuesday, Free. I had never been inside the shop and as I stood there staring at the notice in the window, my wife, Sara asked me if I was okay.

I looked down at my watch and saw that it was 10.20 am. "The meditation class starts in ten minutes," I whispered, a bit dazed. "We have time. Why don't we go in?"

"I guess so," Sara agreed, trying to understand me. Slowly she moved to the glass door and it opened to the sound of wind chimes and soft music emanating from two large speakers hanging on the wall. The music was Native American Indian with which we weren't familiar and caused a strange current in our ears. Not to say that it was uncomfortable, just different. The smell of burning incense smoke lingered in the air and seemed to originate from behind the counter.

There was no one in sight. This gave us time to get accustomed to the surroundings. It was a small shop but filled to the bream. Sara glanced around the room at the rows of books that covered the walls, each section identified by the category, ranging from dreams to the afterlife. A glass cabinet containing crystals of every colour, was sitting under the staircase.

We heard a noise and turned to see a woman appear through a curtained entrance way behind the counter. She introduced herself as Emily and asked how she could help us. I said, "Hello, I'm Joshua and this is my

Chapter 1 *New Beginning*

wife Sara and we were wondering if we're too late for the meditation class."

"Not at all," replied Emily. She was a very attractive woman dressed in a flowing yellow cotton dress. "Kate is ready to start in a few minutes. Go right upstairs."

I hesitated; I think I was trying to think of a reason to change my mind. "How long is the class?" I asked. Emily must have sensed my apprehension and smiled, "It's an hour and you're welcome to come back down to talk to me about your experience, if you'd like," she assured us. Sara moved to the staircase and headed up the stairs.

I followed her up the stairs and we found ourselves in a large room lit only by candles. The sound of birds and soft music engulfed us. The room was sparsely furnished with an old cabinet that held a CD player and a circle of kitchen chairs. About a dozen people were seated already but there were two empty chairs as if they were placed there just for us.

We sat down and it was as if no one noticed us. I became aware that there was only one other male in the group.

"If everyone is ready," said one of the women who I assumed was Kate, "we can start. First, welcome everyone, especially those who are here for the first time." She looked over at us, smiled and nodded. "What I would like you all to do is to sit up straight, uncross your arms and legs, and close your eyes."

I saw both my arms and legs were crossed and I was

already slouching in the chair. I followed her instructions and then let my eyes close and listened to the music with the sounds of the rainforest.

"Next, I would like you to concentrate on your breath," continued Kate very softly. She had a voice that felt like a gentle breath on your neck. "Be aware of your breath and slow it down." I could feel my breath coming in short tight spurts. I forced myself to take longer, more deliberate breaths with a slight pause after each. We practiced our breathing, and after a long pause, Kate continued, "Whenever you find your mind starting to wander, come back to your breath. It is your connection to life, your connection to the Universe. Breathe in. Breathe out. Breathe in. Breathe out. In. Out."

I continued the breathing exercise and suddenly my thoughts went back twelve years to when I had just completed my business degree. I was twenty-one then and unexperienced but determined to become a millionaire before I reached forty. Not a great student, nor talented, I studied hard and managed to get into university.

Like many young men, university was my coming of age. I attended large parties, drank too much and enjoyed the company of women, lots of women. I dealt with my issues by drinking more beer. It was at one of the parties that I met Sara. She took an immediate interest in me and I was thrilled with the attention.

Unlike the youth of today, I did not have the pressure of competing in the job market. Several months before I graduated, I had a job offer at the accounting firm of

Chapter 1 — New Beginning

Molley and Simons, a medium-sized but fast-growing firm in Melbourne. My future was secure. I took the job and three years later, after working long hours, I was promoted to Junior Partner with a substantial raise and more responsibilities. Sara and I were married the same year. The first of our two children, David, was born and I was confident that I could support my growing family. I was working in Ballarat, a small city about a hundred kilometres west of Melbourne, so we bought a house in the same community.

I had a good salary but discovered that with a mortgage and more mouths to feed I was falling behind financially. The house needed repairs and there were additional costs with a growing child. I wasn't prepared for either. The pressure increased and money problems started.

"Remember to focus on your breath," I heard Kate's voice and my attention returned to the present and to my breathing. Where had I gone for a few minutes? And how long was I away? Kate continued, "Whenever you find yourself wandering, come back to your breath. Breathe in. Breathe out."

Again, my mind wandered. This time I had journeyed back a year. I had been so certain when my house was paid off, I would be happy. There would be fewer financial concerns. But by now, we had two children who were both attending a private school and there were some medical issues that required doctor's visits. There was no more disposable income.

I was putting in extra hours at work and missed

seeing my children during the week. I needed to make Senior Partner so maybe one day we could take a much desired overseas holiday. I had always wanted to take the family to Disneyland while the children were young enough to enjoy it, before they reached high school age.

My thoughts came back to the present and I took two large breaths before I drifted away again. It had been a dramatic two weeks, possibly the worst of my life. I had had a checkup at my optometrist about a month ago because I was suffering from eye strain with all the reading of small print and numbers, so I was prescribed multi-focal glasses. It had been so long since I had had a check-up, the optometrist was extra thorough. He tested my peripheral vision several times and it seemed I couldn't see the white ball as it moved out of sight. He was concerned and arranged for me to see an ophthalmologist two weeks later. I waited an hour for a few minutes with the specialist. He ordered a CT scan, just to be on the safe side, he said.

Then I received the phone call that changed my life. The ophthalmologist told me the scan had shown a growth on the pituitary gland that must be removed. "What does that mean?" I asked, hearing only the word growth.

"In laymen's term, you have a brain tumour," he said sounding indifferent. "You have to see a neurosurgeon immediately or you could die."

"What," I stammered, tearing up. "Do I have cancer?"

Chapter 1 — New Beginning

"There's a good chance the tumour is benign, but we won't know for sure until it's operated on," he continued bluntly. "I've made an appointment for you with Dr. Taylor, two weeks from today at 3.00 pm, at his private practice on Drummond Street. It's vital you keep the appointment."

Out of habit, I managed to thank him and put the phone down. Of course, I immediately thought the worst. I had just received a death sentence. This only happens to others, not to me. I'm in great health.

I stood up from my desk and slowly walked over to my supervisor and explained that I had a migraine and needed to go home. I don't know how, but as if on autopilot, I managed to drive home safely.

Sara looked at me when I walked in and could see and feel my distress. She teared up and before I could speak, she asked, "Is it the tests?"

I hugged her tightly. "Yes," I sobbed and told her, "I need brain surgery. The eye specialist doesn't think that it's cancer, but they won't know until they operate."

"You mean he told you all of this over the phone," Sara exclaimed, anger building up in her voice. "Didn't he have the decency to tell you in person?"

"I've got an appointment with a Dr. Taylor in two weeks. I guess we'll have to wait until then."

The next morning, I went to the office and told the principal partner of my diagnosis. The firm immediately decided to put me on sick leave. My life was about to

One Vision

change. I had time to reflect and think about my life and what was important. When faced with the possibility of death your perspective changes and what really matters comes to the forefront.

I went up to our bedroom and I let the tears flow. So often for the next couple of weeks I asked, "Why me?" These thoughts suddenly faded away and I found myself focused again on my breath.

Then something started to happen. My eyes were closed but I sensed that a light was being turned on in the room. I opened my eyes a little and saw that it was still dark except for a few candles burning but the light they emitted was very low.

I closed my eyes and still sensed the light. It was getting brighter and stronger. As I concentrated on this light I noticed it was now surrounded by a series of little lights. Nothing was well defined. But while the lights appeared to be separate, they were connected.

I felt more peaceful than I had for a long time. I had been so concerned about what would happen to Sara and the children if I died. The light was reassuring. Everything was going to be all right. It seemed to be speaking to me and I understood. Suddenly, I felt my grandmother's presence. She had died when I was seven and I couldn't really remember her, but I recognized her now. It was definitely her.

My grandmother and I weren't especially close. I was too young for that, but I don't think that mattered now. There were dozens of lights flickering around her.

Chapter 1 — New Beginning

She was there as spokesperson for all the people in my life who were no longer with me. I started to recognize others. Some I remembered well, while others seemed familiar, but I couldn't recall our connection.

"We are here to support you," my grandmother's voice seemed to call out to me. "If you want to help Sara, stop worrying about her. Stay positive for yourself and for your family." She was saying to me by worrying about Sara, she would worry more, and a cycle would begin that would be harmful in the long-term.

My mind again drifted back into the room and I did a few breathing exercises, but very quickly I returned to the light. I felt so peaceful surrounded by everyone I had known, who were no longer in this world. I felt their love and reassurance.

I stayed there until the light started to fade and as it faded, I heard a soft voice interrupt my thoughts "Slowly, slowly, bring your awareness back into the room. Listen to your breath. In. Out." Then after a short pause, "When you are ready, open your eyes and stretch."

I opened my eyes and looked over at Sara, who was looking intensely at me. Her expression showed me that she knew something special had happened. Silently, we stood up and left the building. We walked to our car in silence. Sara opened the door on the driver's side, got in, and reached over to open the passenger door. "What happened?" she asked, as we put on our seat belts. "You went pale and your lips were moving."

One Vision

"You wouldn't believe it," I said cautiously. "Everything is going to be all right." I told her about the visit from my grandmother, whom I hadn't thought about for years.

"Were you close?" Sara asked.

"I don't really know. I was too young to remember. I think I can remember some events in our lives."

"It might be worth finding out. Is there someone in your family you can talk to about it?"

"I'm not sure," I responded. "They might think I've gone mad. To be quite honest, I'm not even sure what happened myself. All I know is I'm not as scared as I was before."

The trip home was silent. I was trying to make sense of what had happened. But the more I tried to come up with a logical explanation to it, the more confused I became. I realised that I should just accept it for what it was.

When we arrived home, I decided to ring my older sister, Sally. Although we hadn't been close for some time, the news of my tumour had brought Sally and I together and now we spoke on the phone often.

She answered the telephone on the first ring, so I didn't have time to prepare for the conversation. Without any small talk, I described the occurrence to her. She was silent for a moment and then to my surprise she told me that she had a similar experience. Sally had felt this same sensation, about eighteen years ago when

Chapter 1 *New Beginning*

she had almost died in a car accident. She had never told anyone because she was worried that they might think she had a mental illness.

The conversation ended abruptly. That's how it was with Sally. No long good-byes. She always got straight to the point. She had the same experience and she didn't talk about it with anyone. Obviously because she didn't think people would believe her.

Sara and I ate a light lunch. Even though I hadn't eaten breakfast, I wasn't very hungry. I kept reliving the episode and my thoughts ran from amazement to disbelief. I suppose I had already spoken about it with two people to convince myself that it did happen. I realised it might be better for me to talk to my doctor.

I was seeing the surgeon in the afternoon. Sara drove me to his practice because she didn't think it was safe for me to drive. I always did the driving but I was getting used to being the passenger. As we drove, I watched the heavy winds twisting the tree branches, and considered what had happened to me during the two weeks since I had received the devastating news. I had called each of my close friends and told them, explaining I didn't want secondhand rumours circulating. This is how I coped. As I told each person and heard their heartwarming or shocked response, I was absorbing the reality of my situation. I seemed to draw courage from them.

The support I received from family and friends astounded me. Word had spread quickly around the office and my colleagues immediately offered to take over my clients until I was better. I learned the day I left the office feigning a headache, they had already distributed my workload for the next couple of months and I was told not to worry, go home and take care of myself.

It's been a long time since I was at home alone during the day. Sara was working part time at a local centre for disabled children, and I decided to read some of the books on health that friends were already sending me. Books were arriving regularly, with titles like, *"Love, Medicine and Miracles"* and *"You Can Conquer Cancer."* Despite being in shock, I managed to read these books almost at the rate they were received.

Much of the information I read was new to me. Obviously, the subject matter wasn't of interest while I was young and healthy. Various authors described the relationship between body and mind and how our health depended on our emotional response to everything that happened to us. They demonstrated how people were miraculously cured through the power of the mind. These case studies were very impressive. There was the case of a man with cancer who had several operations, including having his leg amputated. His doctors were going to amputate his other leg. When something happened. He refused to listen to his doctors and consulted a naturopath. Through healthy eating, meditation and visualisation, he kept his leg. Three months later, when he went back to his doctor, he was told his cancer was in remission. That was five years ago. Now he was working with cancer patients and helping them heal themselves.

Chapter 1 *New Beginning*

We arrived at the doctor's office ten minutes early and waited more than an hour, reading old magazines. He introduced himself as Kevin Taylor and seemed in a rush. He explained that he was fully booked but he had squeezed me in on the insistence of my ophthalmologist. He wore a brown suit, that would have been fashionable in the seventies and by its appearance, he must have worn it every day since. We sat down in two wooden chairs in front of an antique desk.

He didn't immediately address the tumour, but spoke to me as a professional, and recalled the history of neurosurgery and the exciting advances in medicine since he had started his career. I suppose he was trying to break the ice when all he did was frustrate and intimidate us.

Eventually, he took out two sets of CT scans and clipped them onto an illuminated display panel.

"It appears to me," he started, "you have a large growth attached to the anterior and posterior pituitary gland. Have you been getting headaches?"

"Very few," I told him as I had the last specialist.

"Well, I believe we should operate immediately since there's the possibility you could go blind if the growth presses further on your optic chiasm. How does Thursday sound to you?"

"You mean this week?" I asked, startled.

"Yes, we need to move quickly. I can book you in at St Andrew's for first thing Thursday morning."

With his sense of urgency, panic set in and all I had read in the days leading up to this appointment, evaporated. This was my life, we were talking about.

I sat there dazed as he continued to lecture us about neurosurgery. He said he would not perform the operation through my scalp but through my nose. The instruments would be put up my nose, break through the nasal cartilage and using the latest in medical equipment and computers, including a microscope, he would remove the tumour.

He told me he had made an appointment for me to see an endocrinologist in Melbourne for the morning. Then, in the afternoon, I was to go to St. Andrew's, for more tests. He suggested it would be helpful to do an MRI, but there wasn't much time and it would be very costly, and I wouldn't get reimbursed by my health insurance. I had no idea what an MRI was.

After being uplifted by the books I had read and the many positive stories about people who survived cancer without surgery, I left his office feeling discouraged. I had handed my life over to Dr. Taylor and was feeling vulnerable.

That night, we received a visit from our local parish priest, Father Tom O'Brien. We were regular church goers, but this was the first time he had ever set foot in our home in the eight years we had belonged to his parish. After a clumsy conversation over a cup of coffee, he asked if he could administer the sacrament of the anointing of the sick, or what used to be called 'the last rites.' I said he could. I was open to any help I could

Chapter 1   *New Beginning*

get.

My two children had been coping well. David appeared, on the surface, to be dealing with the situation better than Melissa. At seven, he was taking more responsibilities around the house. He would enthusiastically announce to us after his nightly bath, with his blond, curly hair, wet, "See Mum and Dad, I can wash my hair all by myself." He didn't bother to say he had used a quarter of a bottle of shampoo in the process. Still, he was trying to help. He tried to complete some chores before he would give up and ask for help. He was such a sweet, determined little boy.

Melissa, our younger child, was five and had just started school. The tensions around the house seem to affect her more and she was bed wetting again. This added to the pressure on Sara and getting the children ready for school in the morning, seemed to take longer.

We made a decision, almost straight away to involve the children. I felt this would reduce their worries, at least a little, and prevent their imaginations from running wild. So, they stayed with us while we went through the sacrament of the anointing of the sick, and they looked on in awe as Father O'Brien placed his hands over my head.

Afterwards, I talked to the children, individually in their bedrooms. The walls were covered with the masterpieces they had created at school. I tried to reassure them everything would be all right. I told them I knew God was looking after me as well as them, and in doing so I was reassuring myself.

The next morning, Sara and I took the children to school. We had had very little sleep, thinking about the events of the day and what tomorrow would bring. We had to go to Melbourne, so the children were going to stay with friends for the week. This would ensure their regular routines wouldn't be disturbed. Sara prepared their clothes and packed some of their favourite foods. I hugged them goodbye, telling them I loved them, fearful I might not see them again.

Traffic was slow and we arrived at the endocrinologist twenty minutes late. We were both on edge when I was ushered in and Sara was asked to go to the waiting area.

"Hello, I'm Doctor Henry Gordon. Come in, Joshua," said the large, overweight man in his fifties. "Take a seat." I sat down in front of an antique wooden table, much like the one in Dr. Taylor's office.

"I guess all this must have happened fast," Dr. Gordon said, his calmness was comforting. "I know Kevin Taylor and he's an excellent surgeon. Best all around."

Before I had a chance to say anything, he gave me his perspective on my surgery. He explained an endocrinologist is mainly concerned with the endocrine system of the body; the hormones, and the pituitary gland, which releases these hormones.

"The pituitary gland is divided up into posterior and anterior. The posterior pituitary produces oxytocin. One of its functions is to stimulate the release of milk from the breast after childbirth. The other posterior pituitary hormone is known as antidiuretic, which regulates water retention. This is something that I'll watch for in the first forty-eight hours following surgery. We will be monitoring both the input of water and output of urine to make sure that you do not lose water too quickly."

Before I could ask a question, he continued, "The anterior pituitary regulates the other hormones in the body. There are the thyroid, adrenals, prolactin and follicle stimulating hormones. The last one is associated with the testosterone."

"Will I be sterile?" I asked when I could get a word in. "I read that it's one of the side effects."

"It's possible," acknowledged the doctor, "but we can counter that by giving you a testosterone injection every now and then and put you on cortisone tablets for at least twelve months, or perhaps for life."

"You mean I could be on medication for life?" I protested.

"Things could be a lot worse. We can do more today than we could a few years ago." I hoped not to have to listen to the history of endocrinology. Luckily he continued, "You might also need a nasal spray to control your water retention, as I said, we'll be watching for that."

He spent the next half an hour probing my glands and taking blood samples. He then shook my hand and told me he would check in on me every day while he made his hospital rounds. As I left, I compared what he told me to what I had read during the past week.

Sara and I ate sandwiches for lunch in the park. We often ate lunch because it was lunch time, and not because we were necessarily hungry. Then to relieve some of my tension I jogged around the entire park. Sara sat quietly watching the traffic and people. I had tried during the year to get back into shape by going for a run, every couple of days before going to work. I knew this might be my last run for a while.

St. Andrew's was a large private hospital that specialized in treating patients in need of brain surgery or after suffering from heart attacks. I walked up to admissions carrying a travel bag and gave my name. The receptionist asked a few questions.

"Full name?" Her fingers on the keyboard.

"Joshua Clark Winter."

"Of 204A Eureka Street, Ballarat?"

"Yes."

"Weight?"

"Eighty kilograms," I answered. I had lost over five kilograms since I started running again.

"Height?"

"About one hundred and seventy-eight centimeters, I think."

"Who are you insured with?"

"Australian Unity." I replied looking at Sara for

confirmation.

"Do you know your account will have to paid in full before you leave, which will be about three thousand dollars depending on how long you stay in intensive care. Did Dr. Taylor explain that to you?"

"Yes, I know that," I said, only too aware that would use up most of our savings.

"Please sign here. You'll be in room 504. You can leave your bag here and it will be brought up shortly."

I signed the printout placed in front of me and headed for the lifts. We arrived at the fifth floor and I asked the nearest nurse to point out my room. She led us half-way down the corridor into a private room with one bed and an ensuite. A green gown lay on the bed.

"Please put on the gown as you'll be going downstairs shortly." Her voice was friendly, but authoritative.

She closed the door behind us as I started to undress. I wasn't sure what tests I had to undergo that afternoon. I put on the gown with the back partially exposed. Sara and I were discussing how nice the room was when a nurse entered the room with a wheelchair.

"Hi, I'm Jenny. I will be taking you for your angiogram. Don't worry about the wheelchair. It's standard practice."

"What's this angiogram for?" I queried.

"They need to make sure that blood is flowing

through the arteries in your head properly." Jenny replied, surprised that I didn't know. "The doctor will give you an injection of local anesthetic in your groin so that they can insert a tube into your arteries. It can be slightly uncomfortable."

We left Sara in the room and Jenny took me to a different set of lifts. When we got off the lift, Jenny took me into a large room with a hospital bed in the middle surrounded by large pieces of equipment. She helped me on to the table and then proceeded to lift my gown and shave the right side of my groin area. I knew I had to get used to this and shouldn't feel embarrassed.

Then a doctor entered the room and without even an introduction, gave me a local anesthetic, that left a sharp pain going through my body. He then proceeded to insert a tube into my groin, and manoeuvre it all the way up to my head.

"Have you been told," enquired the unnamed specialist, "that there is a one in two thousand chance of this procedure causing a stroke?"

"No, I haven't been told anything," I replied meekly.

"Well, they should have told you," he said a little too harshly than was justified. He put a drip into my left arm and told me that the fluid would allow him to take clearer pictures.

He walked behind a screen and after a few minutes he called out and told me he would tell me when to hold my breath while he took a series of x-ray images.

Chapter 1 — New Beginning

"Hold your breath now," he called.

I felt an intense pain shoot through my body culminating in something like an explosion inside my head. Still holding my breath, tears streamed from my eyes. I had not expected such severe pain nor had I experienced anything like it before.

"You can breathe now," came the words from somewhere in the room. Tears were wiped off my face. For the next twenty minutes, I had to endure five more waves of intense pain as the machine collected images of my brain. By the end of the procedure, I was colourless and had to be taken back to my room on a trolley, where I immediately fell asleep.

I woke as a trolley arrived with the evening meal. It was only five o'clock. I was given a tray which had several plates covered with stainless steel lids. A plate of sandwiches had been provided for Sara.

Shortly after, Dr. Taylor came in and exchanged a few pleasantries and told me the angiogram had shown my arteries were all clear and I was ready for the surgery in the morning. "Is there anything you want to know?" he asked.

I tried to recall the many questions I thought of, but I had forgotten them all. Then I remembered something I had read in one of the healing books. I asked, "may I have music playing during the operation? I read that it's very good for the subconscious."

"Not a problem, I'm quite partial to classical music myself," came the bemused reply. "Not that you will remember anything during the surgery anyway."

I felt silly asking him, but he didn't seem to mind. Dr. Taylor shook my hand and in a considerate way told me to get a good night's sleep.

Sara stayed with me for another hour and left saying she would come back in the morning, promising she'd be there when I woke up. Sara kissed me passionately and looking at me, said, "I love you very much. See you tomorrow." Her eyes filled with tears and worry, and love. "I love you, too," I replied with all the strength I could muster. We held each other for a moment longer and she left.

I had arranged for a tape recorder to be next to my bed. I had brought with me some tapes of Native American Indian music that I had read would stimulate balance in the body.

For the rest of the night I kept myself busy watching the small television attached to a mechanical arm hanging from the ceiling. Eventually, a night nurse came in and gave me two sleeping tablets. It was the first time in my life I had ever had sleeping tablets. I was soon asleep.

I woke the next morning at six o'clock drenched in sweat, knowing I was being operated on in an hour. I got up and showered before anyone came in. I then sat on the bed and tried to meditate and slow down the rushing beat of my heart. As hard as I tried to focus on my breath, I wasn't having much success.

The door opened and a different nurse came in. She

Chapter 1 — New Beginning

introduced herself as Catherine and explained she was on day shift for the next few days. Her eyes fell on the self-healing books I had brought with me and were sitting on the side table. "Those books are excellent and you'll benefit from reading them." I liked that she was so understanding. She said she always believed conventional medicine combined with alternative practices had better results.

Catherine then gave me an injection in my right buttock, which was going to send me off to sleep. She told me it would take about ten minutes to work and I should go to the toilet first. As I entered the ensuite, I heard Catherine leave the room.

When I laid down on the bed, already feeling drowsy, the phone rang. It was Sara calling to wish me luck and to tell me how much she loved me. I started to tell her I was nervous, but don't remember the rest of the conversation, because I fell asleep.

I woke up outside the operating theatre. An orderly noticed I had opened my eyes and told me that the surgeons were running late. He told me to close my eyes and not to fight the anaesthetic. The last thing I remember was hoping the operation would not change me. The final scenes of *'One Flew Over The Cuckoo's Nest'* flashed before my eyes when a changed Murphy was smothered to death.

Suddenly, I had the same comforting sensation that had occurred at the bookshop come over me. I felt the same loving presence of my grandmother from somewhere above me. I felt safe.

One Vision

I could hear Sara, my sister and my mother's voices nearby. Hours must have passed. They had not been told about the delay and then saw me being wheeled down the hall covered in a bloody bandage. The nurse was comforting them. I had no idea what they were saying but could feel their relief.

"I'm alive!" my mind screamed as I was wheeled past them. "I'm still me."

Awakening

"Imagine white blood cells fighting the after-effects of the operation," I heard my sister Sally, saying over and over. I could hear the sound of Native American Indian music and hospital chatter in the background.

"Look!" Sally stopped, "his eyes are open."

It had been twenty-four hours since my surgery and I was rolled down the corridor. Sally and Sara had kept a vigilant watch; each getting only a few hours of sleep. They had been using visualisations and calling to me, telling me I was well and that my white blood cells were working hard to clear up the effects of the operation.

I opened my eyes and looked up as Sara approached my bedside, with dark bags under her eyes from lack of sleep and worry. "Welcome back," she said, smiling. "We've been waiting for you to wake up."

One Vision

I opened my mouth to speak but nothing came out. The effect of the anesthetic had dried my throat and left a stinging sensation. I groaned and pointed at my throat. I raised my arm, and felt the tube attached to a drip and stopped.

Sara called the nurse, who, looked over my chart, and gave me a small piece of ice. I attempted a smile but found myself slipping back to sleep. This happened a few times for the next few hours. I would wake up, be given a piece of ice, and then fall back to sleep. Each time it was for a shorter period. At the end of the day, I was awake long enough for Sara to tell me that she had spoken with the surgeon. The operation was a success and my pituitary gland was still intact. It was too soon to know if the gland was still working, but at least I still had it.

The next day, I woke, more alert and felt like the past two days had been a dream. I was moved from intensive care to a ward. There was one nurse for four patients. My bed was by the window and I had a view of a small lush garden below.

I had only eaten a few pieces of ice during those twenty-four hours. Now I was given a glass of water and a small bowl of corn flakes. I tried to sit up and felt a sharp twinge in my right leg where, unknown to me, the surgeons had taken a piece of muscle to repair the inside of my nose. The pain brought me back to full consciousness. I felt the drip going into my left arm and I could feel the bandages that covered my nose and forehead.

Chapter Two — Awakening

A nurse was adjusting my pillow as Sara came into the room. After she left, I was able to say, "Good morning."

She smiled, and looked at me with tears in her eyes, "I love you."

"I love you, too," I said smiling.

She told me there were two other people in the ward who had had similar operations. The person whose bed was closest to the door had had the same operation for a third time, because the tumor had come back. It made me nervous and wondered if it might happen to me too.

I went back to sleep, and slept for a few hours, until a nurse came in and asked Sara to leave the room. I recognised her as Catherine, the nurse who had been so kind to me a few days earlier. After Sara left, Catherine removed a catheter I had not noticed and unwrapped the bandages around my head.

"I'm going to take out the bandage from inside your nose," she said, "but I'm afraid it will hurt a little." I could hear in her voice that she was uncomfortable, having to pull the bandage from inside my right nostril. It did cause intense pain, but I couldn't scream. Tears flooded my eyes as she gave a final tug and it was done, and I was able breath through my nose, at least a little.

I decided then there must be better ways to deal with pain. I picked up one of the books on pain management sitting on my bedside table. I opened it randomly and read the first paragraph which suggested we should focus our thoughts on a distant object and that would help block out thoughts of pain. The author pointed out that pain was created in the mind.

This idea motivated me to keep flipping through the book and I started to feel better. When Catherine returned, I told her how much better I felt. She came back later in the evening and took out the drip and I was taken back to my private room.

The next day I slept, meditated and chanted some affirmations that I was going home from the hospital very soon. The surgeon had come to check on me during his rounds and explained I would stay in the hospital for a week and then be transferred to the hospital in Ballarat to recuperate.

The nurses monitored my intake of water and urine output very carefully. The endocrinologist came along and told me the good news that the membrane of my pituitary gland was not broken during the surgery, and I would not need sprays to help me to retain water.

As I lay awake that night, I was aware of the six points where the doctors had entered my skull for the surgery. It felt like nails had been placed there. I decided to meditate again. I was still feeling the effects of the pain killer injections I was getting every few hours, and I was not concentrating on my breath. I simply let my eyes close and watched a blue haze move over me.

Since the day at 'The Silver Tree' bookstore the focus of my meditations was to slow down my heart rate and for me to feel relaxed. The first experience, I put down to shock. Maybe it did not even happen the way I

Chapter Two *Awakening*

remembered it. I could recreate the memory, but not the experience.

Then, as the blue haze lifted, I saw myself in an operating theatre. I was looking down at a body on the table. There were two doctors, an anesthetist and five nurses present. One of the nurses was standing by and monitoring a screen. The colour in the room was brilliant white and I could not see the face of the person lying on the table. Then, it was clear that it was me!

I bounced back into my body and opened my eyes. I couldn't believe I had just seen my own operation! I had heard classical music playing and the shock of seeing my face had completed the vision.

Since I couldn't get back to sleep, I turned on the television and watched whatever came on. It was a show called '*The Extraordinary,*' which told of paranormal occurrences. I had been fascinated by the many unexplainable and strange events, but everything I watched tonight did not appear to be that extraordinary. It all seemed more believable to me.

The next morning, I had just finished describing my experience of the night before to Sara when the surgeon walked in. After his initial examination, I asked him about the six points around the circumference of my skull.

"It's interesting that you should ask about that," he replied, "they are the six points where we used rubber bullets to hold you firmly on the table. I've never had complaints of soreness after surgery before."

From the skeptical look on his face, I decided not to tell him what had happened during my meditation. He had not been receptive to anything I asked him previously, with the exception of playing music during the operation.

The next four days consisted of short stumbling walks. It was difficult to use my right leg because of the cut to my thigh muscle. Friends from work had dropped in and were surprised how quickly my hair had grown back, so I explained the operation was done through the nose. I was improving so much, by the seventh day, I had convinced the doctors to let me go home rather than be transferred to the local hospital.

The next morning, I was taken by taxi to the airport where the surgeon had arranged an air ambulance to transport me back to Ballarat. My stay in hospital had been mostly covered by our private hospital insurance, although it cost us nearly three thousand dollars. I thought it was strange for the hospital to save money by ordering a taxi to take me to the airport, rather than transporting me by ambulance. The plane was scheduled to leave Essendon airport at seven o'clock in the morning, so I had to be ready to leave the hospital with enough time to get to it. I was moved from the taxi onto a bed on the plane. It seemed that no sooner had the plane reached its full ascent than it was preparing for landing at the Ballarat Airport.

This was the smallest plane I had ever travelled on and it was the first time I had seen Ballarat from above. I was enthralled with the view. My hometown was an enormous valley, with a mass of tiled or tin roofs that radiated away from the lake. I looked for my house. But by the time I had a clear view, we were far from where I lived and approaching the airport for landing.

As the plane touched down, my mind turned to my children, David and Melissa. I had not seen them for more than a week and only spoken to them by phone. They had been staying with friends, so they were able to stay in school. Sara's parents had come down from Sydney to help with their grandchildren and Sara left Melbourne a few days earlier to be at home with the children.

I was moved from the plane into an ambulance and taken home. "Please get me home quickly," I implored the drivers, "I'd like to be home before my children leave for school."

No such luck. The ambulance got a flat tyre, and we had to wait fifteen minutes for another one to arrive. They transferred me to the second ambulance, and I was taken home. I arrived just as David and Melissa were getting into our station wagon. They rushed to the back of the ambulance and waited patiently until I managed to climb out. I hugged them close to me, and I thanked the ambulance drivers for bringing me home.

As the ambulance left, Sara's parents welcomed me home and told the children to get into the car and they drove them to school. Sara took my arm and helped me inside. Our bedroom was upstairs so the climb up the stairs was difficult, but I managed it. I got undressed and into bed. It felt great to be home and in my own bed.

After I had stayed in bed for a couple of days, I felt I needed to move. I was going to beat this thing. It was a cool day, I dressed, grabbed my coat, and called out to the children. "Let's go for a walk around the block. I need to start moving again."

I walked outside as the sun breaking through the clouds. With a child on each arm, I started the trek around the block. Even Melissa was patient as I shuffled along. I made it half-way around the block before I ran out of energy and had to have a rest. When we made it home, I went straight to bed and slept for several hours.

After I woke I up I knew I had pushed myself too hard, too soon. I had been a competitor all my life, in school or at my accounting practice. I was convinced I must win because I had learned at a very young age only winners are rewarded. I was always pushing myself and put in long hours at work.

I rested in bed and picked up a book on meditation by Brian Archer. I read his work every day and was meditating four or five times a day. I was still taking codeine pain tablets every few hours, and I wasn't yet feeling the benefits of meditation, but I hoped that over time it would help me decrease the dosage.

I heard Sara coming up the stairs. I had learned to recognise the different sounds of each family member's footsteps on the stairs. She came in to tell me she had heard on the radio that Brian Archer was speaking in Ballarat in two days' time, on behalf of the Cancer Support Foundation.

"I think it would be good for me to go," I said quite excitedly. "I've just been reading more of his book."

"Do you really think you could do it?" replied Sara concerned, "it will be a long day."

"What if I call you when I feel I need to leave? It's not every day someone like this comes to Ballarat. Besides, don't you think it was a coincidence, I just happened to be reading his book as you were coming up the stairs?"

We agreed I could go, on the condition that I wouldn't push myself as I had done yesterday with the walk around the block. The workshop was scheduled from ten in the morning until four in the afternoon.

On the morning of the workshop, when I arrived at the conference center, I was surprised at people's reaction to me; I was aware I still looked like someone who was recovering from an illness. The organisers immediately escorted me to a chair in the front row.

People around me were introducing themselves and explaining what had brought them to the workshop. Some were there for personal reasons while others were practitioners and wanted to improve their practice. There were about a hundred and fifty people in the room. The trip had already tired me out, so I tried to relax before engaging in conversation with the people sitting beside me.

Then Brian Archer walked in and sat down on a chair in the middle of the stage in front of me. People were clapping enthusiastically, and I noticed he seemed slightly underweight and moved slowly as if he was mindful of each step.

As the applause died down, he spoke in a quiet but clear voice, "Welcome everyone and thank you for coming. The fact that so many of you have turned up means you see the importance of meditation in your life.

"Meditation is simply a state of being. There are many books which discuss different approaches to meditation but there is no correct way of meditating. In actual fact, the simplest and most effective way to meditate is to use no method at all.

"However, our mind is always trying to distract us when we try to still it. How many times have you tried to meditate when all you can think about is whether or not you have turned the stove off or what you will have for dinner? Maybe you are sitting quietly but all you can think about is your nose is itchy. You just have to scratch your nose and as soon as you do, you're itchy somewhere else. That's just your mind trying to stay in control."

I could certainly relate to what he was saying. How many times had I tried to sit quietly in the past and found my mind went over unimportant day-to-day events or I was thinking about a conversation I had had with someone earlier?

Brian continued, "Certain methods, therefore, can be a good starting point for those of us who are easily distracted and find it hard to still the mind. After a period of time, you may find you can stop using these methods or you only have to use them occasionally.

"So today, I am going to show you some of the methods you can use to help you start meditating or improve your meditations. Remember though, the best meditation technique for you is the simplest one that works."

He paused and took a bottle of water from under his chair and took a sip. "Now, before I begin, can everyone check their posture? When you meditate you should be in a symmetrical position, whether sitting in your chair or lying on your bed at home. Avoid crossing your arms, unless you are intentionally sitting in a yoga position. Do not slouch. Sitting up straight prepares your body and mind to calm down.

"You must also maintain your body temperature. Your temperature will drop during a meditative state, so I suggest that you cover yourself with a blanket before you begin. The first method I will show you is called the progressive muscle relaxation technique. Now I want you to take a large breath in through your nose and out through your mouth. Again, in through your nose and out through your mouth." He asked everyone to close their eyes and repeated the breathing exercise several times.

"Now, I want you to concentrate on your right toes. When you breathe in tightly squeeze your toes and relax them when you breath out. In, squeeze your toes. Out, relax. Again breath in, squeeze, out, relax."

He then asked us to do the same for our right foot,

One Vision

right calf muscle and right thigh before repeating the procedure on our left legs. I was already starting to feel calmer and more relaxed, and had recovered from the stress of just getting to the workshop.

We continued squeezing and releasing various parts of our body, from our buttocks, stomach muscles, chest, arms, hands and finally aspects of our head. As I squeezed my eyes, I felt the tensions around my face. After allowing us time to just enjoy the quiet space we were in, Brian asked us to slowly open our eyes. I stretched and noticed that everyone around me was doing the same.

Brian took another drink of water and continued, "The purpose of this method is to distract the mind. When you're focused on contracting and relaxing your muscles, your mind is otherwise occupied. After you do this for several weeks, you'll find that you'll get the same results without the need to contract the muscle. Week after week you will be able to focus on fewer body parts. For example, instead of relaxing your legs, you might focus on just your feet and toes. You can then do the same for the body, arms and head. Finally, you'll be able to relax your entire body at once. Of course, you can always go back to different stages and do what works for you. Your attitude is as important as the steps you take."

Brian continued to describe several other methods, such as just focusing on our breath. He asked us to close our eyes to observe our thoughts and try not to control them. Interestingly, as I became an impartial observer and started to watch my thoughts, they disappeared.

Then Brian asked us to concentrate on the gaps between the thoughts.

"Another method you could try is to concentrate on one thing at a time to calm a busy mind. You can concentrate on the image of a candle, a white light or an object that is significant to you. You can repeat a mantra, focus on your favourite music, or count your breaths. Each can bring about a quieter mind."

A female voice from somewhere in the room interrupted his train of thought, "Excuse me, Brian, but when I'm meditating, I find myself getting light-headed and feel like I'm falling. I become scared and quickly come out of my meditative state. Can you suggest how I could avoid this?"

Brian was not at all bothered by the interruption and was happy to answer the question. "The main reason for mediation is to help us deal with stress. At the beginning you'll find that it relaxes you and you feel warm inside. You might see colours or get flashbacks to things that happened to you in the past. This is all normal. Then sometimes you get to a point like you have just described. At that time, you might ask yourself, should I keep going or do I stop? Fear sets in and it's the fear of the unknown when many people will stop. Sometimes fear comes because they believe meditation is against their religion. Or a hundred other fears might get in our way.

"In answering your question, what's important is you trust the process. You must have faith in a god who's protecting you. Many begin their meditation with a prayer. Personally, I begin my practice with the 'Our Father'. Choose whatever prayer is the most meaningful for you.

"Finally, whenever you find yourself getting stuck, return to your breath. Concentrate on each breath rather than on the fear. When you can do that, you'll be able to break clear.

"You'll find that once you break clear, two things may happen. First, you'll find yourself sitting with a still mind within an infinite space. Here you don't need to do anything, but just be still and be. It is a wonderful, natural space.

"Second, you may experience visions or even out-of-body experiences. By this, I mean you may come outside of yourself to find the answers you have been looking for or to find new directions. Either way, you will learn more about yourself.

"I think now is a good time to stop for lunch. We'll continue in an hour and give you enough time to get some nourishment and to get to know each other."

Everyone stood up and headed over to the room near me where sandwiches and drinks lined the table. I realised that this was the longest time I had been awake since my surgery, and I was starting to feel tired. Brian noticed my discomfort and came over to me.

"You look like you're in some pain," he said with concern and sat down next to me. I briefly told him about the tumour and that I had been reading his book when my wife informed me he was holding this

Chapter Two *Awakening*

workshop in our city today.

"You know," he said looking straight into my eyes, "the same thing happens to me. For some reason, I always seem to meet the right person at the right time. It often happens when I'm centred on myself because of some difficulty I'm dealing with and need help."

I told him the story of our experience at the 'The Silver Tree,' that we were walking by and found their meditation session was starting within minutes.

"Life's like that," Brian comforted me, "I think that sort of thing will happen to you more and more often. I feel you're coming from a very good place."

His comments made me feel better and I shared with him, I was still in a lot of pain despite spending the morning meditating. He told me there must be a balance between this complimentary approach to medicine and the more conservative approach.

"In other words," he reiterated, "it's okay to still take some form of pain killer if you need it. Hopefully, you'll be able to take less and less with meditation." With that, he excused himself and went to lunch.

I got up and took some more codeine and had a light lunch. I met a woman who told me she was here because her mother had been diagnosed with cancer. She had come with her whole family, to support her mother's search for alternative ways to heal. Not being close with my mum, I was glad to hear about her close family.

I decided I was up to staying until the end of the

workshop. The codeine had reduced the pain and I was in a happy place, a place that I needed to be.

Promptly at one o'clock, the participants were called back to their seats, and Brian picked up where he had left off. "Many people use imagery to meditate on. Rather than trying to still the mind, they create a story and focus their attention on a journey, combining meditation with visualisation. Visualisations can be used to achieve a goal. It can be a goal about getting healthy, improving a relationship, or finding a job. To achieve a goal, you must be clear about what it is. Be realistic and make sure the goal is achievable. Know what you want and be prepared to adjust your goals as circumstances change."

It was important for me to hear this. I had set myself a goal to be back at work in two months. I was already home from the hospital much sooner than I, or anyone had expected, and I was determined to do even better. Sara always said I was too competitive.

"Let's get back to visualisations," Brian continued, "There are three general types of visualisations. The first is to use analogies. For example, if your goal is perfect health, you might visualise yourself having little "Pac-men" figures inside your body eating up the viruses and infections.

"Another is to visualise that you have already achieved the goal. For example, think about your doctor telling you, your cancer is completely gone. Or, you see yourself and your family celebrating that you are completely healthy.

"Finally, there is an abstract visualisation, where you're feeling your breath moving through your body clearing away the illness. You could also focus on a colour or a mantra and keep repeating what you want.

"Our natural state is to be healthy. We can maintain this natural state by caring for our body and our mind. Meditation and a healthy diet are only two of the activities we can do to care for ourselves. It's when we don't take care ourselves that we get run down, get sick and fall into depression.

"Depression is the opposite of being happy. Most people believe they will be happy sometime in the future. They will be happy when the house is paid off. They will be happy when a certain relationship improves. Or any number of things outside of ourselves. I suggest to you, your happiness can happen today and not at some abstract time in the future.

"When our body, mind and spirit are in their natural states, we are happy. Meditation is integral to that happening. It can help you clear out obstacles such as grief, guilt or fear and replace them with more positive emotions like hope, faith and love. It can also help move you towards finding answers to those core life questions, 'Who am I?' or 'What is my life's purpose?'

"I want to caution you, go easy on yourself. Many people try too hard to meditate. Yes, you need to be committed to doing meditation but do not take it too seriously. Enjoy it. I was meditating once when I started to laugh, and I got the whole group laughing. I don't even know why I was laughing, but the more I tried to stop myself, the funnier everything seemed. I guess what I'm trying to say is have fun and don't take yourself too seriously.

"Before I continue, are there any questions?"

A gentleman behind me asked, "How much time should we allocate to meditating?"

"The answer to your question is there's no correct answer. It's up to you. I meditate one to three times a day. I suggest you just start with once a day. Those who say they don't have time to meditate are really saying they won't make it a priority. Perhaps you could spend less time watching television or take one less coffee break and use that time to meditate.

"You can meditate for ten minutes or an hour. I think starting with twenty or thirty minutes would be a good goal. You should try to meditate in the same place each time. Perhaps your bedroom. People like lighting candles which help to calm the mind. And of course, please turn off your phone. Make sure that you're in a peaceful environment." He paused and looked around the room to see if there were any more questions.

After a short pause, I raised my hand and when I saw Brian turn towards me, I said, "I just started to practice meditation and I do it because I've read it can reduce pain. But sometimes, as I get into it, I find that I'm actually in more pain. Can you explain this for me, please?"

He looked at me and smiled. I could see that he was very empathetic and was trying hard to honestly answer my question. "At the start of our practice the act of preparation will be a little stressful and our mind isn't completely relaxed. The pain will fluctuate. We'll feel less pain at first and then because there are no distractions, it will increase. When this happens, focus on your breath concentrating on the place of your pain. You will find after a few deep breaths you'll have less and less discomfort."

I had already tried this and sometimes it worked and at other times it did not. I picked up my pen and wrote on my notepad, "BREATH INTO THE PAIN".

Other questions were about commercial meditation tapes and group meditation sessions, like the one Sara and I had attended at the bookshop. Brian emphasised that meditation was an adventure and these options were personal choices on how and where to practice. There are as many ways to meditate as there are people. Some people mediate while they run, others meditate while working in the garden and others may mediate while listening to music. For the rest of the day, Brian taught us several methods of meditating. The one that appealed to me was when we imagined we were going to die in two months. He asked us to list the five things we wanted to accomplish before we died. I realised everything I listed had to do with my family. I wanted to spend more time with them, to express and show them how much I loved them. Brian then asked us to imagine ourselves doing everything we listed. He ended the exercise by reminding us, "You could die tomorrow so set your priorities and work towards them each day."

What happened to me during the past few weeks had

certainly changed my priorities and I understood now that whatever happened, I would continue to examine and adjust my behaviours. My life was going in a different direction and something special would happen as a result of that. I never felt more peaceful and positive.

When the workshop ended, I wanted to go up to Brian and personally thank him for his advice and help. However, a crowd immediately cornered him, to buy his book and get him to autograph it. I was thankful to have spoken with him during lunch and made my way to the car, where I knew Sara was waiting for me.

As I walked to the car, I noticed I was limping. My thigh muscles had tightened where some tissue had been removed. I didn't notice the man in front of me and bumped into him. It was the optometrist, Greg Westbrook, who first referred me to the other specialists. It took me a minute to recall his name.

"It's good to see you," he said after we both apologised for bumping into the other. "I've been wondering how you were. I wanted to let you know about some new therapies, so come back and see me, if you're interested in learning more," he said, and walked away.

On the drive home, I described the events of day to Sara. It was good to talk to her about something other than what I was feeling since the operation. I told her I had just bumped into my optometrist and he suggested I make an appointment to see him about my eyesight.

Chapter Two *Awakening*

I rested for the next few days. The day at the workshop had been long and tiring. I learned a lot and was inspired to do more but found it difficult to maintain the positive outlook and, of course, I was still relying on codeine for some relief from the pain.

The pain and depression were worse at night. I would have dreams or even nightmares of the operating room. I would watch as the doctors were securing me to a device to keep my head from moving and could feel the effects of the aesthetic. Sometimes I would wake Sara at four o'clock in the morning to talk or I would go downstairs to try to settle the fog in my brain and subdue the pain with my mind. Sometimes it worked.

Sara's parents had left for home two days after I came home from the hospital, so Sara had been left on her own to take care of the children and me. As much as I tried not to be a burden to her, I was more dependent on her than I would have liked.

It took me a week after Brian's workshop, to take action. I had read an article in the local paper about something called Reiki. It was some sort of spiritual healing that helped balance the bodies energies. I wanted to limit the amount of codeine I was taking and decided to give Reiki a try. I had nothing to lose.

It was a Tuesday morning, and the children were at school and Sara had gone shopping. I called the phone number in the newspaper. The woman who answered the phone introduced herself as Martha Brooks. After hearing my story, she told me she became involved in Reiki after her husband was diagnosed with cancer.

I felt she understood my situation and I did not feel embarrassed for having reached out for something that might help me. Martha explained she did not do house calls, but she was going to be in my neighborhood later in the afternoon and could come to see me. I agreed.

Martha arrived in a rusty blue station wagon that was at least twenty years old. She appeared to be in her mid-fifties and was wearing a glossy orange tracksuit made from parachute material. Her brown hair had a touch of red in it and was done up in a bun, on the top of her head. She took a folded portable massage table from the trunk of her car.

After she introduced herself at the door, she entered and made her way to my lounge room, where she set up the table. "Reiki," she began to tell me as she was setting up the table, "is the process of using energy to balance the body. The healing takes about one and a half hours. As I told you on the phone, I charge thirty dollars for my time. The energy is free. Is that still all right with you?"

"Fine," I replied, bemused a little by the situation. Martha told me to lie on the table on my back and asked me to close my eyes. She started with my feet and placed her hands against the soles of my feet. I sensed a feeling of warmth, first at my feet where she had placed her hands and then the sensation travelled up my legs and eventually I felt warm all over.

After about five minutes, she moved her hands, one at a time until both were on my knees. Much of the sensation of heat shifted from my feet to my knees. The process had relaxed me in much the same way as the progressive muscle relaxation technique that Brian had introduced in his meditation workshop.

She was moving her hands up my body. I became less and less aware of her hands and was only noticing them in my mind. I had lost track of time when I felt her hands over my eyes. The image of the operating room came to mind as it did most nights. Then it disappeared and all I could see was the color green.

After a few moments, the picture of the operating room came back again, as white as it always looked to me. The room embodied fear for me. I saw people in white preparing to operate. Everything in the room was white and sterilised.

Then suddenly I thought about the colour green. Why not place green plants around the operating room to cheer it up? I started to place huge green ferns throughout the room in my mind. Everywhere I looked, I put potted green plants to overcome the starkness of hospital white. Then I heard myself chuckle and knew this hospital scene would no longer disturb my nights.

Just as Martha was finishing, Sara arrived home, surprised to see a massage table in the middle of the room with a strange woman placing her hands all over me. She sat down and waited for our session to end.

After I had paid Martha and she had left, I talked to Sara about what had happened. She seemed less concerned than I expected and told me she would support whatever I needed to do to feel better. That

One Vision

night, I slept through the night for the first time since the operation.

Doorways

The next day, two of my work colleagues visited and told me not to rush back to work. They reassured me; my clients were being taken care of well. I was a bit concerned that I wasn't indispensable, and I could be so easily replaced, even in the short term. I was glad I was getting such support, so I relaxed and did not feel the urge to get back to the accountancy firm.

But I did feel the need to read the books I had discovered. I was fascinated by the way in which Martha used energy. The closest I had ever been to this before was when I had taken David to a chiropractor to deal with his episodes of head banging. Whenever David was disciplined for doing something wrong, he would sit on the floor and bang his head. Disappointed by the advice of doctors that he would grow out of it, Sara suggested a chiropractor whom she heard could cure the problem by manipulating the spine and skull.

She had suggested this behaviour may be the result of David being born by caesarean section.

I remembered after each manipulation, the chiropractor would lift her hands about ten centimeters above David's body. I had mentioned this to Sara, suggesting she may be a witch doctor, the way she waved her hands all over David. That was two years ago, and David had not banged his head since. So, my perspective on these different modalities of healing was changing.

Martha had suggested I have another session, and I told her I would call if I thought I needed it. I was now considering trying many different approaches to healing. I looked up Dr. Michelle Heart, the chiropractor who had treated David and called her. Coincidentally, she had just had a cancellation for ten o'clock the next day and I took the appointment.

I arrived promptly at ten o'clock. I noticed things had changed somewhat from when I was in a doctor's office, a while ago. The staff were now assuming they had a right to keep their patients waiting and not apologise for wasting their time. I was surprised that Michelle remembered me, and she asked about David. I was happy to report back to her that he was fine and she had helped him.

"I hear you're not well," she said as I sat on a chair next to her desk.

"Yes," I replied, wondering how she knew and who had told her.

"I was talking to Greg the other day," Michelle replied, anticipating the question. "He's been keeping an eye on you by making enquiries to your doctors. He's concerned."

"Yes," I said, "Greg found a tumour on my pituitary gland and I had surgery to remove it a few weeks ago. I have been doing a lot of reading while I'm recuperating."

"What types of books are you reading?"

"Obviously, mostly about cancer. I know what I have is not really cancer, but I have not found many books about benign tumours. The surgeon did say there was a good chance that another tumour would regrow on the same spot."

"I see your point. Did you find the books helpful?"

"It's certainly been a new way of thinking for me. I had not considered anything like meditation and self-healing in the past. Perhaps, because I didn't have the need." I stopped to think about the question and continued, "I think what I've learned is I need to take responsibility for my health and take charge of my life rather than leaving it in the hands of doctors when I get sick."

"How do you feel about doctors now?" asked Michelle.

"I'm not really sure. All I know is I walked into the hospital feeling well after going for a nice, long run and came out feeling sick. I actually think the doctors made me sick."

"But you did have a tumour before you went into the hospital. You must know the doctors played an important role. It's a matter of balance. That's what I try to do here. I help your body maintain a balance."

"I tried Reiki the other day and I felt so much better after my session but then last night I again started to feel sick again. I woke up at four this morning with my head hurting and some terrible thoughts." I was remembering those thoughts now; returning to work, feeling sick, the surgery and even, dying. While each thought lasted for a few seconds, the feeling lingered much longer.

Michelle considered what I had told her, and said, "What you need to remember is you have just had a major operation and it will take time before your body can get back to normal. My experience has been it can take up to twelve months for the after-effects of the anesthetic to wear off, let alone the effect of the pain killers that you're taking."

"I'm still taking codeine when I'm in a lot of pain." I said.

"A lot of what you're experiencing at night is a direct result of the codeine. It can put you into a semi-illusionary state. You have to consider how much pain you can live with before deciding to take more codeine. It's a very addictive drug, and you may already be addicted to it. Try to reduce the amount you're taking now or take another painkiller sometimes to cut down and eventually stop using it altogether," Michelle advised, seeming quite concerned.

I realised then that was exactly what was happening. I would take two tablets before I went to bed and I would wake up in the morning feeling spaced out. I would continue to feel this way until I got up. I would meditate and while it helped a little, it didn't eliminate the problem.

"What I suggest we do today," Michelle continued, "is carry on clearing away the effects of the operation. It should make you feel better."

I took off my shoes and laid down on the table on my front. Michelle told me I didn't have to remove any clothing. Michelle began by moving her hands up and down my body, even though she did not actually put her hands on me. I knew where they were by the strange warmth I felt on that area.

Then, Michelle put both hands at the top of my spine. She did something that felt like a twist and a cold shiver ran through my body. I knew she was doing some form of chiropractic manipulation. Her hands moved down my spine until her hands rested on my coccyx bone. After she worked on each side of my body, she told me to sit up slowly.

When I was sitting upright, Michelle told me she did not make many chiropractic manipulations, but instead used Chironic Healing, which helped clear out toxins. The use of Chiron, she said, worked on the etheric level, which was the energy field that surrounds our bodies. It worked on several levels. Today she worked on mending the gaps in my aura which were caused by the operation.

I was somewhat comfortable with her explanation but wanted to know more about this energy field and who were the best practitioners in this field. She acknowledged my skepticism.

"What you have achieved in the past few days is extraordinary," she said. "You have taken the first steps on the journey to take control of your life. By coming to see me, you've demonstrated you are open minded and willing to explore alternative ways to get healthy.

"It's important you take things slowly. I don't expect you to fully understand what we did today or to believe it. That will take time. What I did is for your physical health and to create a balance between your mind and body. If you'd like to learn more, we offer classes here a couple of times a year.

"Now you need to rest. Don't expect to recover quickly. Give yourself time to adjust to the changes your body is experiencing and just go along with it."

I was pleased she understood what I was feeling, and that I was still trying to beat all records in my recovery. I was still coming to terms with my situation and I needed to slow down. I was planning to go back to work in a few weeks because I was concerned the partners might think I was taking advantage of my situation and taking off more time than I needed. Sara had warned me I should slow down, but I had refused to listen.

When I left the building, I had a slight limp. Michelle

had suggested I get a massage. I'd never had one before, so it seemed like a good time to try something new. The tumour had given me the opportunity to experience new ways of healing.

The practice was only two small blocks from Lake Wendouree, but I wasn't driving on my own yet, so I decided to start out by walking and stopped along the way to pick up a salad roll for lunch. I would have to take public transportation the rest of the way home.

Lake Wendouree is a picturesque place that was home to the 1956 Olympic rowing competition. The five colored rings of the Olympics have been standing there as a memento for more than forty years. I had been on my school's rowing team and had rowed on the lake as a teenager and came to see it only as a sporting venue not the elegant swan-filled centre-piece of the botanical garden. I had always been too occupied with rowing or running its six-kilometer circumference, but on that day, I saw the gardens as if for the first time. The flowers were in bloom, and the air was vibrant and alive. I walked around the lake and enjoyed the gigantic lush trees that surrounded it. The lake was a striking blue. It was spring.

I sat and ate my lunch slowly, enjoying each bite. I felt good and I thanked God I was alive. The sun was brighter, and there was a wonderful fragrance in the air. The tumour seemed to have opened my eyes and I saw the life I had planned for myself was going to be different. I had started on a new journey, as Michelle had implied.

My enthusiasm seemed to wane a bit as I grew closer to home, and I made a conscious decision to limit the amount of codeine I was taking. Instead I would meditate to help relieve some of the pain. For the next few days, I did take less codeine and kept meditating. I found I was thinking more clearly at night and, while the pain still woke me up, I didn't feel as disorientated. My friends started dropping in and while they did not stay too long, my days were fuller.

I started to share some of my experiences about Reiki and Chiron with my visitors, but after receiving a few blank looks, I shared less and less. They told me they were surprised I looked so healthy. I was also surprised I hadn't heard from some of my closer friends. I considered they may be concerned that my condition was contagious or perhaps I reminded them life was not forever.

I wondered if I had done something and I mentioned my concerns to Sara, who reassured me that it was their problem. I went back to see Michelle the following week. I told her I was getting stronger since I was taking less codeine and in the past two days, I had only taken one tablet. I also told her my friends were surprised by how well I looked in spite of my surgery.

"Sounds like you're starting to see it too," she said, looking happy with my report.

"Yes, since I have reduced the amount of codeine I am taking, I don't feel sick. I still tire easily and have a nap during the day, but I think I'm ready to go back to work," I told her.

I felt Michelle was truly listening and understood me. "You should understand there's a difference between being sick and being ill. When people get the flu, they are sick. They look sick. Everything about them shows it.

"But you are ill. It might not be obvious on the outside, but you can feel it. It takes time for your body to recover. Think about your surgery like a heart attack. It can take six months to recover from a heart attack. The same applies to your recovery."

I had not looked at it in that way. I knew a heart attack was serious, but I was thinking my operation had been a minor surgery. After all it was just a small growth.

At that moment I gave myself permission to be ill. I started to cry as relief flooded my body and I knew I could take my time to get better. This realisation was significant.

Michelle handed me a tissue and I climbed on to the table. After the session, Michelle gave me a small bottle. She explained it contained flower essences that would help repair the damage caused by the operation.

As I put on my shoes, she smiled and gave me a look of satisfaction like a teacher who is pleased with her student's progress. "You're doing really well," she said as I was leaving. "Keep learning. We're all here to learn."

I slept very well that night. In the morning, Sara reminded me, I had an appointment with the surgeon later in the day. I was due for a check-up, to see how I was progressing since leaving the hospital.

I had been told one of the effects of taking cortisone is weight gain, so I was watching what I ate. Being in the house all day, I was tempted to eat too much. All I had to do was open the pantry door. I would eat even if I wasn't hungry. I never had much time to eat at work and sometimes I would just have a snack at lunch time.

I decided to try to relax before my trip to the surgeon and fell asleep for a while. Sara was planning to leave work earlier than usual to collect me for my two o'clock appointment. I half-jokingly told her, she might as well come at four as the doctor was sure to be running behind time. That afternoon, Dr. Taylor took us into his room just twenty minutes short of my four o'clock quip. He was wearing the same suit he had worn when we first met him almost a month ago and every day in the hospital. As we sat down, my mind was flooded with memories of that experience and I became uneasy.

Dr. Taylor was completely unaware of my unease, and he continued talking at us, beginning where he had left off a month ago about the history of neurosurgery. This time I wasn't prepared to listen and interrupted him.

"What happens next?" I asked abruptly.

He stopped and looked at me, surprised. He then proceeded to check my vision, my glands and examined my nose, probably to check his handiwork. "How have you been feeling?" he asked.

"Sore," I said, not wanting to get into it.

"I recommend you get your hormone levels checked by Henry Gordon in the next few days. And then I'll arrange for some radiation treatments for you."

This was the first time radiotherapy had been mentioned. I immediately saw myself going bald. "Why are you suggesting radiation therapy?" I said, my voice barely audible.

"The only options we have right now are radiation or chemotherapy, and in your case, I think radiation is the better choice. I'll have to book you in for an MRI first."

"What's an M.R.I.?" I asked, feeling the energy draining from my body.

"It stands for Magnetic Resonance Imagery and gives us a better picture of your brain than a CT scan. You'll lie on a bed and go into a tunnel where magnets are used to take pictures of your brain and show us if there's any residual tumour."

I became agitated. "In that case, let's wait until after the MRI results before *you* decide what to do next. The tumour may be gone," I said as I decided not to tell him about the visualisations I had been doing to clear away the tumour.

"You're right, there's no urgency, but I think you'll have to have radiation therapy at some point, so I thought it would be best to do it sooner than later. Then your hair will grow back sooner too. But if you want to wait until after the MRI, that's fine with me," he said, sounding comfortable with my suggestion.

I had changed course from the original recommendation of the doctor. I was taking control and responsibility; to be honest and realistic about my illness for my wife and children. It was my future and I had to reclaim my power.

Three days later, I travelled to Melbourne to see the endocrinologist who took several blood samples and told me I could reduce the amount of cortisone I was taking. Two days later, I learned the test results were clear and my hormone levels were within the normal range. Although, I didn't know for sure if normal levels were where I should be.

While in Melbourne, I also visited a doctor who specialised in nutrition. Without even discussing my present diet, he suggested a multi vitamin tablet containing selenium made by a specific health food company. When I went to buy the tablets, I saw the nutritionist was on the board of directors of the company that produced the pill. I did not think this was ethical, so I stopped buying the recommended brand of tablet. In my opinion, this was definitely a conflict of interest. During the next few days my emotions fluctuated. I was up and down but I noticed I was up more than down. I also received a doctor's certificate to stay off work for another two months.

I was scheduled for an MRI a week later. It seems getting an appointment for this procedure could take several months, but my surgeon had scheduled the MRI immediately after my operation, so I didn't have to wait

Chapter 3   Doorways

now. I hadn't had one before the operation because of the cost. It would have cost me a thousand dollars for the procedure, and there was no government rebate. I still didn't know what an MRI was and couldn't find any information in the literature I had around the house. A college friend suggested that I watch a film called *'The Doctor'*. I asked Sara to borrow a copy of the video at the local video store and I watched it a few days later. It was about a doctor who learns he has throat cancer and his experience changes his attitude towards his patients. The film showed the doctor being transported headfirst into a cylinder as he underwent an MRI. It was strange to learn about a medical procedure from a movie. The following week, Sara and I drove to Melbourne. We felt uneasy when we arrived at the hospital car park. "Are you okay?" Sara asked me as I slowly got out of the car.

"I have a fear of hospitals since the operation." I replied, looking up at the tall building. "Fair enough," Sara said sympathetically.

We found a receptionist who gave us directions to the imaging department, and we arrived there about ten minutes later. The woman sitting behind the desk looked like she'd been working there forever. Next to the piles of paper, I could see a computer screen and I noticed that it was turned off. Technology hadn't yet caught up with this person. She appeared to be unwilling to use it.

We waited anxiously for about forty minutes then I was given some hospital 'greens' to put on. I was taken into a room and asked to lie on a hard table with a device that held my head firmly in place. The operator remotely slid the table into the huge machine with an opening just wide enough to allow my body to fit in.

As I lay still with cotton wool in my ears, I heard a message from outside the tunnel. 'Hold still now, Mr. Winter. The first set is about to begin." I heard what sounded like two rocks hitting against each other as the magnets took the photographs. The noise was quite deafening even with ear plugs and I focused on quieting my mind.

The noise got louder and faster for several minutes and then paused. This process was repeated three times, with each session lasting for about ten minutes. I was taken out of the machine and had a drip containing a dye inserted into my arm. I was told that the dye would help make the pictures clearer. Then I was slid back into the tunnel for another ten to fifteen minutes. There was more noise in the cramped conditions of the tube but by the end of the second session I felt more relaxed.

"You look very much at ease," the attendant said as he removed the drip.

"I was meditating to help me stay still," I said, attempting a smile.

He looked puzzled and rephrased what I said. "In other words, you were in an altered state of consciousness," he said, pleased with his understanding.

"You can say that." I didn't see any need to contradict him and it really didn't matter what we called it. "I don't think the dye you've used here was as bad as the one I had for the CT scan. That one made me quite ill."

"Most people find this easier than a CT scan. But it's different for each person. It can also be different every time. Hopefully, your experience has been all right should you need to have it done again."

I did feel a little lightheaded, but after eating lunch I was much better. We had to wait for the results before we headed home. On the way I decided I should see my optometrist, Greg Westbrook. I found I was not wearing my glasses in the morning and the length of time before I needed to put them on was getting longer. I also did not feel I needed such strong lenses anymore.

When I called his office the next day, I was told I could come in at any time. So, I scheduled an appointment for the following day at five o'clock in the afternoon, the last scheduled time for the day.

I had a follow up appointment with my neurosurgeon, Dr. Kevin Taylor, the following Tuesday, when he was in his Ballarat office. My mind was on the MRI results and I found my energy depleted as I waited for the doctors' advice.

I spent my time before the optometrist's appointment resting and reading. As I was getting ready to go, I wondered why I felt a need to see Greg right now, while I was distracted by other things. Was I being vain, or could it be I noticed my eyesight had improved? I had been wearing glasses since I was sixteen. I was so engrossed in these thoughts I did not realise I had stopped worrying about results of the MRI. Sara and the

One Vision

children drove me to the optometrist and then went to do some grocery shopping. Melissa and David yelled, "See you, dad," as Sara drove off.

I walked towards the front door of the optometrist's building and stopped to look at my surroundings. There had been a lot of buildings restored in the city, but there was still much to be done. The overhead power lines were an eye sore, as were the large billboards on the building tops. But I was pleased about the improvements being made to my city.

Greg was at the receptionist's desk as I entered the waiting room and they both greeted me, and the receptionist asked after my health. I told them both I was feeling a lot better as Greg ushered me into his office. I noticed the uncomfortable, backless chairs, the trolley of lenses and an eye chart behind the door. Then, my eyes fell on a shelf of cassette tapes and books. I saw that some of the books were ones I had been reading and was surprised Greg would have them at his office until I remembered I had last seen Greg at the meditation workshop. He was also searching.

I sat down on one of the chairs and Greg asked me to remove my glasses and hand them to him. He looked carefully at my lens and made a note on his pad. Then he turned off the lights and the room became totally dark. He then turned on another light that shone on the eye chart directly in front of me. He put an eye patch on my left eye.

"Which line can you read?" he asked. His voice seemed professional and unemotional.

"I think the top letter is an 'A'. That is about it," I said, hesitating as I felt my shoulders tighten.

He put a device over my eyes and moved different lenses over it. "Which one is clearer, one or two?" he asked. "Two," I said. He continued this same process a few more times and then moved on to my right eye. But with my left eye, I couldn't see anything clearly. He removed the device and the test was completed.

"I've found your glasses are too strong for you. We'll reduce your lenses from -3.75 in the left eye to -2.5 and -3.5 in the right eye to -2.25 and supplement the difference with exercises and relaxation techniques." Greg said, surprisingly.

"Will I be able to see better?" I asked, too focused on the numbers rather than the idea of retraining my eyes.

Greg replaced the eye patch on my left eye. "What do you see now, Joshua?"

I could see the 'A' on the top line more clearly. "I can read the 'A' and the next line is 'D, F'."

"Very good," exclaimed Greg, "Now take a few deep breaths and relax."

I did as I was asked and noticed I was blinking more. I looked at the chart and I could read the second and even third lines and only when I reached the line beginning with 'S' did the letters start to blur.

"Well done!" smiled Greg. "The relaxing and

breathing helped you see better. With a little more practice, you'll see more lines.

"If you broke your leg, you would not expect to be in a cast forever. You would expect your leg to heal and with exercise you know you would be walking in about four to six weeks. The same can be said about your eyes. Why is it when people receive their first pair of glasses, they do not expect to come back in six weeks and have the optometrist tell them, they no longer need their glasses? What happens is when they come back in a year or two, they're told they need a stronger pair of glasses."

He was saying something rarely heard from optometrists. "I've been doing this job, prescribing glasses, for fifteen years. But no one I've examined has ever seen better over the years without stronger and stronger glasses. No one has ever thrown out their glasses. I've been telling people unless they wear their glasses, they're eyes will deteriorate even more. That's what I've been taught.

"I've noticed too often, after wearing their first pair of glasses, people come back and tell me they're getting headaches. I just tell them to be patient, they will adapt to wearing glasses and the headaches will go away. But I think what happens is the eyes do adapt to the stronger prescription and get weaker, and this goes on year after year.

"Maybe optometrists need to look at eye care differently. You demonstrated you could improve your eyesight by relaxing and taking a few deep breaths. I think people feel stressed when they come in for their eye test and the test results show they need stronger glasses. I suggest if I give you a weaker prescription, you can retrain your eyes. I have a book here with some good exercises to help improve your eyes. I want to lend it to you."

He hesitated, not wanting to force me to do something with which I didn't agree. "Of course," he stressed, "it's your decision."

I was pleased with his recommendation. He was allowing me to do things differently. At the same time, I wanted someone, a professional, to tell me what to do. I needed time to let these options sink in, so I told Greg I'd give him my decision soon.

When I was young, everyone in my family wore glasses at one time or another. Since I was the youngest in my family, I just assumed I would be wearing glasses at some point because weak eyes were hereditary. So, it came as no surprise when I found myself borrowing a friend's glasses to see the blackboard.

I remembered my brother, Paul, asking his eye doctor for a prescription for contact lenses when he was eighteen to be told contact lenses were for vain people and that he did not need them. A few years later, I also tried wearing contacts, but I ended up with an infection and stopped using them. I thanked Greg for the book and left. I think we both knew I'd be back soon to let him know if the exercises helped improve my eyesight. Sara and the kids were waiting for me in the reception area. On the drive home, I told Sara about my checkup and she was enthusiastic and thought it was a good idea for me to focus on something else while I was recovering.

The next day was a sunny day so I decided to go for a walk. My thigh muscles were still sore, but I wasn't limping anymore. I decided not to wear my glasses, since the park was only a few blocks away. There were several sporting ovals surrounded by trees and a four-kilometer running track that marked the perimeter of the park.

As I walked along the path, I noticed a sign for a health center on one of the residential homes. In all the years we lived in this neighborhood, I had not noticed it, so I decided to take a closer look. I could barely read the sign from across the street since I was not wearing my glasses although I seemed to be more aware of my surroundings without glasses.

I crossed the street to read the sign. The health centre specialised in massage. I remembered one of my doctors suggesting massage would aid my leg's recovery. I had already tried Reiki and Chiron, so why not a massage, I thought. I noticed this was not a house, but two homes joined by an elegant verandah and surrounded by pristine gardens. Inside the building was the same. It was well kept, with expensive ornaments covering the shelves on the walls.

A woman in her mid-twenties, in a pale blue uniform, was sitting at a desk. She stopped writing and looked up. "Can I help you?" she asked politely.

"I'm thinking about getting a massage," I replied, "Can you tell me how much it costs and how long it will take?"

She was very pleasant, "The massage sessions are from a half hour up to an hour. Twenty dollars for 30 minutes and $30 for an hour. Most private health insurance companies will cover the cost of the massage."

I told her I had insurance and asked if there was an appointment available.

"I don't have any appointments for the next two hours," she said and introduced herself as Jenny.

She took me into another room where she asked me a few questions about my health and filled out a form. I told her about the operation and that my leg had been giving me trouble. After she completed the questionnaire, she asked me to remove a few pieces of clothing and lie on my stomach on the massage table then she left the room. I didn't know how much clothing to take off, so I called out to her. "Oh, sorry," Jenny said, "I need you take off everything, down to your underwear and lie down on the table with your head in the hole at the end of the table. There are a couple of towels on the table that you can put over yourself if you're cold."

The room was quite warm, so I undressed, then laid down on the table and clumsily placed the towels over me.

Jenny came back and switched on a tape of very

gentle music. A wonderful fragrance emanated from an oil burner. She fixed the towels and asked if I was comfortable. I raised my head slightly to see her putting oil on her hands. She removed the towel that was covering the top half of my body and started massaging my back. The oil smelled of lavender that I had been adding to my bath. She seemed to touch all my sore points, and I was becoming more and more relaxed. She had a gentle voice and was making some idle chatter which was distracting; I would have preferred to just relax and drift off to the music.

When she finished my back, she replaced the towel and lifted the other towel from my right leg. She proceeded to work on it being very careful near my skin graft. She spent a lot of time massaging my leg with gentle pressure. She said it was too soon to do too much work on my leg. She then re-draped my right leg and started to massage my left leg. Jenny stopped at what must have been an hour and told me I could lie there for a few minutes to relax before getting up and getting dressed. Then she left the room.

I felt very relaxed in spite of her constant chatter. I was glad I had decided to walk in and ask for an appointment. I stayed for a few minutes before getting up and dressing. Jenny came back with a glass of water which was very refreshing. "Take it easy and drink plenty of water for the next twenty-four hours," she told me as we made our way back to the reception area.

I paid her and walked out into the sunshine feeling very peaceful. On my walk home I reviewed all the recent experiences and advice I had received from the doctors and practitioners I had seen, especially the information from Greg. I was learning so much. My illness had opened doors to some valuable learning experiences.

One Vision

A Different Way of Seeing

I see myself standing in a room filled with people. I'm answering questions about who I was, what I have done and where I see myself in a few years. I feel very comfortable answering the questions as if public speaking is natural to me. I see my reflection in the mirror at the back of the room. The beard I had grown after the operation is gone. My hair is shorter and despite the grey around the edges, I look younger. But the most interesting part of the picture is I'm not wearing glasses.

I woke up as I was about to answer another question and realised I had been dreaming. The dream was so real. I rarely remembered my dreams but lately I often did and quite clearly too. I stayed in bed for a while and thought about the events of the previous day. I had had a call from Kevin Taylor, and he had told me the MRI showed the tumour was still present and suggested another operation. The second procedure would be followed by a new type of therapy called focus radiotherapy. He said it could be done at a hospital in Sydney and was so advanced the equivalent of four weeks of treatment could be done in one day.

He also explained the MRI showed the tumour had spread into the optic chiasm where the optic nerves intersected. Unfortunately, I hadn't had an MRI before my surgery because of the cost, and the CT scan had not picked this up. He said this would need to be a cranial operation to remove the tumour and any residual pituitary gland.

I was determined to avoid another operation, so I asked if the tumour was growing and he hesitated. He said he didn't really know, so I suggested a course of radiotherapy first. Then another MRI to see if the tumour had shrunk before I underwent another surgery. Surprisingly, he agreed and told me he would send the MRI results to Sydney to see if they agreed with this plan.

It was now August, and it didn't seem I would be going back to work any time soon. I had accumulated plenty of sick leave during my time with the company, but I would have liked to have been back to work on a part-time basis by now. I was thankful I had a doctor's certificate until the end of November.

Knowing I was going to be home for a few more months and having seen myself in my dreams not wearing glasses, I decided to work on improving my vision.

Chapter 4 — A Different Way of Seeing

I slept well that night because of my earlier walk and massage. Sara took the children to school and went to work. When I woke up, I stayed in bed and picked up the book Greg had given me. It was on my bedside table next to a growing collection of books. I turned to the vision exercises, and read:

'The first vision exercise is palming. This exercise uses the energy that emanates through your hands to create healing in your eyes.' I wondered where this energy was coming from, before continuing. *'You can do this sitting comfortably in a chair or sitting up in bed. If in bed, put your elbows on pillows so you can use both hands to cover your eyes. Now, rub your hands together several times, close your eyes and cover them with the palms of your hands. Make sure you don't touch your eye sockets. Focus on your breath and the energy radiating from your hands. Focus your thoughts on your eyes and imagine your eyesight getting clearer and more vivid with each breath.*

You can do this for one minute or for thirty minutes combined with a meditation practice. When you're done, slide your hands down and gently dab the balls of your eyes with your fingers. Remove your hands and open your eyes slowly. You should notice improved clarity.'

I put the book down and placed two pillows under my elbows. I glanced at a poster on the wall adjacent to the foot of my bed and had trouble reading any of the words. I then followed the procedure and palmed for about two minutes. When I covered my eyes, everything went black but I saw shooting streaks of light. I assumed

One Vision

the white streaks of light was my healing energy.

When I opened my eyes, I looked over at the poster and read, 'Beautiful Victoria'. The words appeared clearly for about ten seconds and then they began to blur and as hard as I tried to restore the clarity, I couldn't. But, as they say, I had seen the light.

Now I was excited. I picked up the book and read the next chapter, which was entitled, 'sunning'. I skimmed the section which explained what I needed to do, then I got out of bed and showered. I dressed warmly and put on a brown cap. The sun was bright but there was a cold breeze blowing from the west. I decided to just sit on the verandah for a while.

I closed my eyes and recalled the instructions in the book.

With my eyes closed, I looked up at the sun and felt the full power of the sunlight. I moved my head from side to side allowing the sunbeams to drape over my eyes from every angle. I did this several times and could feel the energy envelope me. I felt somewhat silly trying to 'look' at the sun with my eyes closed, but when I finished the exercise and opened my eyes, the colours of the trees and flowers were so much brighter and clearer.

For the next few weeks, I worked on improving my vision. I would palm each day and sometimes I would meditate and palm. When the sun was shining, I would do this outside and when it was cloudy, I'd visualise myself sitting outside in the sunshine thoroughly enjoying the warmth of its rays on my face. I was

Chapter 4 — A Different Way of Seeing

keeping a journal and recorded how much time I was outdoors and the length of time I didn't wear glasses. I found I was wearing my glasses less and less; usually I would take them off after wearing them for about ten minutes and I was seeing more clearly without them. I was also recording other observations in my journal. I had noticed I was becoming easily frustrated when I was looking for something and couldn't find it. I think what I was feeling was fear but I didn't know of what. There seemed to be a connection between wearing my glasses and my emotional state.

At first, I put it down to coincidence. Then I realised it was happening all the time. I was feeling angry, fearful and anxious. I also recognised my eyesight was no longer improving. I could wear my glasses more often or I could look at what was causing the decline. Like many people, I had never considered why I was wearing glasses.

That night, I focused my meditation on my childhood. I slowed my thoughts down using the breathing exercises and centred my thoughts on the school yard. I saw myself the day after I had been given my first pair of glasses and considered what my life was like around that time. My eyesight had not deteriorated overnight. As I thought back, I could see this was the time when my parent's lives were unravelling although it wasn't until a few years later when they finally separated. Those years were difficult for all of us. This had been a new insight for me.

The next morning, I took the vision chart from the book and went outside onto the verandah. I asked Sara to come outside and test me. When I looked at the chart, I was able to read most of the twenty-fifty lines with both eyes, which was a hundred per cent improvement. I was thrilled and wanted to tell Greg right away.

As I picked up the phone, Sara asked, "Why do you think there's been such an incredible improvement?"

I thought for a moment before I answered, "I can't be sure, but I have been doing some vision exercises and also meditating on what may have caused the weakening of my eyes in the first place."

"I understand what you're saying," she replied, confirming my own feelings. "I believe there is a strong connection between physical and emotional trauma. I'm sure stress is the main cause of illness. When we're stressed our brains are sending messages to rest of our bodies saying, sort out your problems. But most of the time we're too busy to listen to ourselves and we'll get the flu or something even worse, to make us slow down.

"Look at the changes in yourself since the surgery. You're more relaxed and so open to new ideas. You may not like what I'm about to say, but I think the tumour has been good for you."

Sara was right. My life was moving in a different, more meaningful direction. The reality was when I had started to work on improving my eyesight, I had found something that distracted me from worrying about my other medical problems.

I called Greg who was just about to take his lunch break. He was very excited for me and invited me to come to his office, so he that he could see my improvements for himself. For the first time in months, I drove by myself to the optometrist's office, feeling very confident in doing so.

I arrived at Greg's office and he carried out the test right away. I read the entire twenty-fifty line and part of the line below it correctly. "That's remarkable!" Greg exclaimed, quite surprised. "If you can see all these lines, you really don't need glasses and you can remove the notice on your driver's license."

"Can you explain to me what twenty-fifty and twenty-forty actually mean?" I asked.

Greg sat back in his chair and turned the lights on. "Twenty-twenty is what optometrists consider to be normal vision. It means you can see letters of a certain size from twenty feet away. If you cannot see at twenty-twenty that's an indication that your eyesight is weak.

"The last line you were able to read and see on your test today was twenty-forty. That means the size of the lettering on the line is twice as large as the lettering on the twenty-twenty line. When you first came in, you were reading at twenty-two hundred, in other words, ten times the size that you should be able to see from twenty feet away."

"The indicators of what you can see, from today's test, means your eyes are working to about seventy-five per cent efficiency. At this rate, I'm sure you will be able to get to one hundred per cent if you continue doing whatever you've been doing."

At times, I knew I was seeing beyond seventy-five percent, but I couldn't really prove it. When I tested my vision, I could see while it was very good initially, a few minutes later it deteriorated. I realised part of the problem was my stress levels increased when I wasn't achieving what I thought was optimum results. Still, I had proved to myself that there continued to be measurable improvement with my eyesight.

The same night, I decided to write some goals for myself. The first one was to be able to drive without glasses within two years. The second goal was to be free of the tumour at my next MRI. As I became more and more excited about the improvements to my vision, I was less concerned about the tumour. Then I was told the specialists in Sydney did not want to do the focus radiotherapy treatment because the tumour was too close to the optic nerves.

I had mixed emotions. I was disappointed because I knew this decision increased the need for another operation but I was also more determined to work on my own healing.

Greg had just purchased a machine that used coloured lights to help heal the body. We decided to see if the lights would work on both my tumour and my vision. I would have a twenty-minute session with Greg every morning at nine. He would put me under the indigo lights; ten minutes for the pain and another ten minutes to reduce the swelling.

The next morning, I arrived promptly at nine, pleased to be driving myself again. After yesterday's test, Greg

Chapter 4 — A Different Way of Seeing

explained to me I had recovered about ninety percent of my peripheral vision and it was safe for me to drive.

I sat in the darkened room in front of a machine that reminded me of an old-fashioned movie projector. Greg turned the machine on, and it produced a rainbow of colours ranging from a deep ruby red, through the fourteen colours of the light spectrum, to violet.

"These colours," Greg explained, "are associated with the autonomic nervous system. The reds, oranges and yellows affect the sympathetic nervous system that stimulate the body. This is where the term 'fight or flight' comes from as it increases your heart rate and blood pressure. The blues and purples relate to the parasympathetic nervous system, that slows down the body, at times when we're resting or digesting food. Green is in the center of the light spectrum and is a balancing colour."

I imagined the colours of the rainbow; red, orange yellow, green, blue, indigo and violet. Even though the colours blended into each other, green was always in the middle. Greg continued, "The colour turquoise is in between green and blue, and it can balance the effects of the operation, which is still at the acute stage. The indigo should help relieve swelling."

After ten minutes, I was skeptical. I did not feel any noticeable change, but I decided to complete the session. I thanked Greg and left the office. As I arrived home, I felt a wave of tiredness enfold me. I laid down and slept for four hours.

One Vision

Afterwards, I awoke feeling refreshed and decided to do some more vision exercises. I read the next exercise in the book which used beads on a string. I found Sara's sewing basket and cut a piece of thread about a metre long. I discovered two cards of buttons, one with five red buttons and the other with five blue buttons. I wondered where she had bought them and why. I tied the buttons onto the string at even intervals, alternating between red and blue. Afterwards, I tied one end of the thread to the side of Sara's dressing table. I sat on the edge of the bed and put the other end on the tip of my nose so the string was straight and perpendicular to my face.

I focused on the first red button. I noticed the way I had attached the buttons to the string had caused an X to appear exactly where I was looking. When my eyes focused on the fifth, red button, the X moved to that button. My eyes refocused on the first button and saw a V forming, as if there were two strings of buttons. My eyes continued to move up and down the buttons for about ten minutes. I noticed it was difficult to maintain focus past the seventh button. I couldn't see the last blue button clearly, but the end of the string formed a V as I tried to focus on where I had fastened it to the dressing table.

After my first attempt at this exercise, I was sure with daily practice, my sight would improve. I added this information to my journal along with records of the vision exercises I did and how long I spent doing each one, daily. I was also recording the strength of my lens prescriptions. As I reflected on my notes, I could see I

Chapter 4   *A Different Way of Seeing*

was going longer without glasses and when I needed to wear glasses I was using the ones with the lower strength lenses.

I began with the beads exercise each day, using either the string of buttons or just my thumb. I would stretch my arm and thumb out and look into the distance. I would see two thumbs similar to seeing two strings of beads. Then the harder I would focus on my thumb, it would become just one, but with the impression of seeing double. By the middle of October, I was spending at least twenty to thirty minutes a day doing vision exercises. I also devoted time to palming while I was meditating or listening to a visualisation tape. The visualisation tape had the sounds of the rainforest on it. As it guided my meditation, my vision became perfect and I would see myself wandering along a path through dense trees and green ferns. I could smell the fresh air and feel the leaves under my feet as I strolled up the mountainside. As I completed the walk in my mind, I would drift into a peaceful sleep.

I was using the various visualisations Brian Archer had taught at the meditation seminar I had attended several months ago. I would visualise just before I fell asleep. I would imagine what it would be like to have perfect vision. However, the most empowering visualisation for me was the one where the white light was flowing through my body, healing me. Each time I practiced this visualisation I felt energised. I would wake up and say an affirmation. At first, my affirmations focused on the physical, something along the lines of, "My vision gets clearer every day." But lately, my affirmations were becoming more emotionally charged. This morning, I said, "I trust the truth in what I see." It had been a few weeks since I had noticed any improvement and I was becoming disheartened, so the next day I went to talk to Greg.

"I'm not sure this is working anymore," I told him.

Greg understood I was pushing myself and I wanted to see faster progress. "Be patient. You're doing well. Give yourself time to adjust."

I was being told I had to give my eyes time to adjust to every small change. It was part of my recovery. "What do you mean by adjusting? What should I be doing?"

"You've shown tremendous discipline in staying on the program and you've seen consistent improvements. Now you have to expand what you understand as vision. When people say, 'men of vision' they're referring to more than what you see on an eye chart.

"Joshua, I've seen some interesting changes in you since our first meeting. Back then, you were living in your head. You took everything I said literally. I did too. We're both changing our perceptions and being more trusting and more intuitive now." I understood what Greg was saying. Formal education suggests people who are good academically are the truly intelligent ones. Mathematics is not intuitive. I wanted to belong to the intelligent group and clinically analyse everything in the same way Dr. Spock did on Star Trek. I lived life in my head and chose a career in accounting, where every

Chapter 4 A Different Way of Seeing

problem had a solution. I had never done anything illegal, but I knew how to work the system to my client's advantage. It was all in the timing. I pushed myself to be the best and the fastest in solving problems.

But during the last four months, I had been making decisions based on instinct rather than logic. The time I spent working on improving my vision felt good. Logically, what I was doing should not have been possible. I was enjoying the process, including keeping a record of the slightest improvement.

"But now, I'm not seeing any improvement," I repeated. "Yesterday, I put on my full-strength glasses for the first time in weeks and I could see so much better."

Greg was sympathetic. "Yes, I can see you're discouraged, but how did you feel while you were wearing the stronger glasses?"

I considered his question, "Actually, I did think things looked almost too intense and I felt a bit of a headache coming on," I said.

"So, what do you think about it now?" asked Greg, pleased with my answer.

"Not as bad, I guess. It's difficult not knowing if what's happening and what I'm feeling is consistent with my experience. I could use someone to talk to who understands."

Greg interrupted enthusiastically. "As a matter of fact, there is someone you should go and hear. His name is Andrew Whitecross. He's coming to Melbourne from the United States on November 1 and I plan to go to hear him. I'll send you a copy of the flyer and, if you like, you can come with me."

For the next two weeks, I doubled the amount of time I spent doing vision exercises and made notes of what I would want to discuss with Andrew Whitecross. He would be in Melbourne for only a day, so I hoped I'd be able to talk to him.

Greg had volunteered to help set up the room for the presentation, so we left Ballarat early. On our drive to Melbourne, Greg explained that Andrew Whitecross was a pioneer in the use of colour light therapy for vision correction. "His approach to light therapy is called Syntonic," Greg said. "The word Syntonic comes from 'synonym' meaning 'to bring into balance'. For a long time, it was believed that the colours of the rainbow corresponded with the energy centres or chakras in our body. As you know, the red end of the spectrum stimulated the body while the blue end slows it down. I work with these colours.

"But new research shows it's possible to use specific combinations to treat certain conditions. For example, with you it was indigo to reduce pain and turquoise to reduce acute swelling. Andrew changes the vibration of each colour by strobing the unit at various flash rates. He's created new ways to use the colour machine."

This was new and interesting information for me. I believed my regular twenty minute sessions on Greg's colour machine had been beneficial. I would not know for certain until I had another MRI which was scheduled for later in the week. We were arranging the chairs around the room when Andrew arrived. He was staying at the motel next to the conference centre. I saw him as he walked by the window. Behind him I could see the Westgate Bridge, leading to a congested Melbourne street. When Andrew came in, I decided to introduce myself before the other participants arrived. I waited until he sat down on one of the green, plastic-moulded seats and walked over with my list of questions. Before I could open my mouth, he looked up and his eyes seemed to settled on me.

He had blue eyes, the colour of the ocean. "You must be Joshua," he said. "Greg told me you were coming. I have been looking forward to meeting you." I sat down, and before I could reply, he put his right hand on my chest and spoke softly, "You are very strong, Joshua. At times, too strong. You're safe here. Live in the present."

I was taken aback. Yes, I was trying to drive my own recovery and improve my eyesight at the same time. I was sure I could do better but now Andrew was giving me permission to slow down and be in the moment. I felt safe. I couldn't think of anything to say and nothing I would have said would have been appropriate in that moment.

I took a deep breath, stood up and walked over to Greg. "What do you think of him?" Greg enquired.

I looked at the list of questions in my hand and ripped them up. "I had all these questions about what more I should be doing ready to ask him. After meeting him and getting his advice, asking them would be pointless." I said and we both laughed.

"He had the same effect on me. Great, isn't it?"

At the seminar, Andrew told us he became an optometrist to prove he could do it; that he was smart enough. As an optometrist he had kept increasing the strength of lenses for both his patients and himself. Then he had started to question why people never came back with improved eyesight. It seemed their eyesight was always getting worse. So, he had begun to experiment on himself and within a year, he no longer needed to wear glasses. "Everything changed for me one day, when during a meditation session, I could see everything in the room clearly though my eyes were closed. I knew the location of every piece of furniture and could see the paintings on the wall, including the signature at the bottom.

"When I opened my eyes, the room looked exactly the same as when my eyes had been closed. It was as if a cloud had been lifted from my eyes and since then my vision has been excellent."

I was thinking if what he was saying was true, I too, could achieve perfect vision. I was certain I was going in that direction. I looked around the room and saw Michelle Heart, a friend who had also travelled from Ballarat to hear Andrew. She seemed totally absorbed by Andrew's lecture.

I was feeling good and realised if it wasn't for the tumour, I wouldn't have come today. The lecture and

Chapter 4   *A Different Way of Seeing*

the discussion that followed was enlightening for everyone present. After the meeting, Greg and I drove Andrew to the airport. His next scheduled speaking engagement was in Sydney. I made some clumsy conversation comparing Australian and American sports.

On our drive home to Ballarat, Greg asked me if the trip had been worthwhile and what had I learned. "I appreciated my conversation with Andrew and what he said to me personally. He told me to live for today and how important it was to be loved and to love myself. He urged me to take responsibility for my health and to stop blaming myself for things beyond my control." This was the first time I had discussed love with anyone other than Sara.

I had the second MRI the following week and I waited patiently for Kevin Taylor to give me the results. I felt confident I was doing all the right things to rid myself of the tumour. Despite this, as I started my meditation and vision practice in the morning, I felt some anxiety.

When I was taken into the doctor's office, I asked him to be honest and direct with me. "The MRI shows the tumour is stable. It hasn't grown at all. Based on these results, I suggest we do nothing and get another MRI in six months," he said, adding there was no reason to have another operation.

After leaving the building, I felt Dr. Taylor still didn't accept what I was doing was helping with my recovery. I wasn't confident I could destroy or even

One Vision

shrink the tumour. I felt defeated until I realised the results I had received were certainly better than if the tumour was growing larger. At least, from my perspective, things were going in the right direction. The doctor said because of my progress, I could stop taking the cortisone, which meant I would be off all medications.

As things were improving, I decided I would like to go back to work in the coming weeks, at least for a few hours on a couple of days. Sara and I met with my partners and they asked her if she felt that I was ready to return to work. After considering Sara's positive response, together, we decided I would rejoin the company for four mornings a week until the end of the year. Then we would assess my progress to see if I could do more. I had already decided I would never return to full-time accounting work.

I spent the next two weeks relaxing at home as if I was on vacation. Sara and I were planning to take the children away for a few days, but as the time drew closer I didn't feel up to traveling. There was an alternative music festival in Ballarat on the same weekend, so Sara and I decided to go to that instead.

Sara was taking an interest in my collection of new books. She was starting to recognise the merit of the different ways of thinking I had been sharing with her. We would regularly bounce ideas off each other and sift through processes or exercises that were working for me. We were also becoming open to exploring new ways of looking at things we had previously taken for granted.

Chapter 4 *A Different Way of Seeing*

We dropped off the children at their friend's house and went to the festival. The event was being held in a park and by the time Sara and I arrived, it was crowded with people who were curious about or enjoyed alternative music and healing. We walked along the row of tents stopping at some that were exhibiting new healing methods. There was a long line waiting for the tarot card reader. We found two stalls that were offering Reiki healings and Sara decided to have a session. Afterwards, she told me she was impressed by the energy she felt from the woman who had simply put her hands on her shoulders. Sara suggested we go our separate ways for a while so she could continue to have a look at the stalls and she would meet me near the food tents for lunch.

I thought this was a good plan because I was most interested in those healers who might help me with my vision. I decided to try a massage first. A group of people in white jackets were offering neck and shoulder massages for five dollars. I sat down on a massage chair and put my face through the round opening. A male masseur started to squeeze my shoulders and rub my neck. He said my muscles were tight, and I shared with him I had been doing self-massages to help improve my vision. He was very helpful and suggested how I could do a better job. He said there were certain acupressure points around my eyes and temples that I could massage to relieve eye strain. "Don't press too hard," he cautioned and demonstrated the ideal amount of pressure.

"Other important acupressure points are in the back

of your neck and are called the occipital points. You'll know you are in the right spot when you feel a little bump. These points are also linked to vision. Place your thumb behind your head, push up and hold." He demonstrated the movement on me as he spoke and I felt a sharp pain. I groaned, and he reduced the pressure.

I thanked him. I actually thought I was seeing a bit better already. Next, I moved to another stall, where a man of about forty was wearing blue jeans and a t-shirt with the word Kinesiology printed on it. "What is that?" I asked, not even trying to pronounce the word.

"Kinesiology is the science of muscle activation. We look at the body's balance and if it's out of balance, and most people are, we use energy to rebalance it. We treat the whole body. We don't fix a disease or try to eliminate symptoms. We restore the body's balance and then the body fixes itself," he explained.

"Are you saying that you can tell if I'm sick by testing my muscles?" I asked.

"Not quite," he smiled. "What I'm saying is by testing the muscles in your arm, we can identify how much you're body is out of balance. Let me show you. Sit down and put your arm out in front of you."

I sat down and stretched out my arm. He placed his hand on my wrist and gave several gentle pushes. "What's your name?" he asked.

"Joshua."

Chapter 4 — *A Different Way of Seeing*

"Alright then, please say, my name is Joshua."

"My name is Joshua." As I said it, he pressed on my arm and it locked in position.

"That's a hold. Saying your name hasn't caused you any stress. Now I want you to say, my name is Fred."

"My name is Fred." As I said the words, he pushed on my arm with the same amount of pressure as before, and it dropped to my side. "What happened?" I asked.

"Your muscles reacted with stress to the false statement. It couldn't support the lie and became weak. In the same way, we can use muscle testing to help rebalance organs, glands and the whole body. We are more than our physical parts. Kinesiology works on your whole being: physical, emotional and spiritual."

It was fascinating to see how my arm responded by staying strong or becoming weak and falling away. He continued to test my glands and organs to see if they were in balance. He picked up on the pituitary gland and told me it was very much out of balance. I told him about the surgery, and he explained there was scar tissue damage and that was causing me stress.

It was getting close to noon, so I thanked him and went to meet Sara. We exchanged our experiences. She had listened to a talk on aromatherapy and had bought a bottle of lavender oil. She told me she learned one should use only naturally made essential oils and not those that were chemically produced as they had little healing qualities.

One Vision

We ate a delicious vegetarian lunch and continued to explore the stalls for the rest of the afternoon. It was certainly more interesting to listen to these practitioners rather than read about them. We had enjoyed the afternoon but all too soon it was time to collect the children.

Since I was now preparing to go back to work part-time, I spent more time working on my eye exercises and was noticing a lot of improvement. I could clearly see the beads on the string. I tested myself reading the eye chart again and my results were very good. I could read all of the twenty-twenty line and even some of the letters on the twenty-fifteen line. I was very pleased, so I called Greg. He told me he would come around to my house during his lunch break.

I was still doing my eye exercises when he arrived. He took out some cards with letters on them. I read each of them correctly. He then tested each eye and found I was seeing at twenty-twenty five with my right eye and twenty-thirty with my left.

"You can now legally drive without glasses, Joshua. I'll fill out a form for you to take to the vehicle registration office. They will remove the eye restriction notation from your license. Well done. You've corrected your eyesight in less than six months."

I wanted to celebrate so I drank a light beer. Immediately, I noticed a change in my vision. Things were less clear. Not by much, but I could tell the difference. Our diet apparently has a role in how we see too. I knew an achievement of twenty-twenty on an eye chart was not the end of my journey. I had more work to do and I was going to continue, I just didn't know what else I had to do.

I went to the vehicle registration office later in the afternoon and the attendant said he had never performed that task before and wasn't sure how to remove the information from my license. I filled out some forms and he issued me with a new license free of charge. I went home and to celebrate took my family out for dinner, wondering if the food would affect my eyesight. This was not something I would have even considered in the past.

At the end of November, I went back to work part-time, and I left my glasses at home. My colleagues all said I looked different but couldn't say what it was that made the difference. They asked if I had had a haircut or if it was my health. After working for a few hours I was tired and happy to go home and take a nap. The partners had not given me a lot of work, and suggested that I take my time getting back into the routine. Things seemed to move fast in the office, especially compared to the slow pace I had been used to at home for the last five months.

My workload did increase by mid-December. By this time, I had changed my work hours to two and a half days and I was planning to go to four full days in the new year. I was looking forward to a ten-day break at Christmas. Christmas Day, this year, was particularly special. We celebrated with Sara's parents and I had thanked God I was still alive and improving every day. It had been a challenging year and I looked forward to seeing what the coming year would bring.

One Vision

A Different Way of Doing

New Year's Eve was a busy time, and our street was bustling with people going out to celebrate. We decided to celebrate at home with the children. I certainly did not want to go out drinking. I had not given up drinking, but I had cut down a lot for my own well-being.

The children were young and were going to bed early, so we moved the clock forward in order to celebrate the end of the year and the start of the new year, ahead of time. David and Melissa were both very happy to think they were staying up late and after a few cheers and a half-hearted attempt at singing *Old Lang Syne*, Sara and I took them up to bed and they fell asleep quickly.

Sara suggested we spend the rest of the evening meditating. I lit a candle in our bedroom and put a few drops of lavender oil in a burner. There was a lot of loud partying near us, but our room was very quiet, and we were able to relax and go within. I felt my body vibrate as I moved into a deep space. A few minutes later, I had a vision of two men on horses galloping, one behind the other. I saw one of the men was me and the other looked like he was chasing me. I was on a white horse, wearing clothes suited to Robin Hood and his merry men. When the man pursuing me caught up, I fell off my horse and hit my head on a rock. When I awoke, I was lying on a bed in an otherwise empty room. A woman was attending to my head wound, and I did not know if I was going to survive.

Midnight came and the sound of cheering brought me out of my trance. I kissed Sara and told her about my experience. "What do you think it means?" I asked.

"It seems to me," she said, "that you were in an altered state of consciousness. I'm not sure what your vision means. Did it feel real or did it feel like a dream?"

"It certainly felt very real. I even felt pain when I fell off the horse. It seemed like a memory from my past, but I've never been on a horse. I wonder if this was symbolic or I should take it literally."

"Given you had this experience now, it must be related to the new year, so you'll get an idea of what it means in the coming year."

I thought about what Sara had said and we both decided to set an intention for our meditation sessions. Not since the day at 'The Silver Tree' had a dream felt so real.

Chapter 5 — A Different Way of Doing

Sara and I talked about the events of the previous year. We had certainly started a different personal journey since the phone call last July. I asked her to tell me how she was feeling and if she was coping with our crises.

"In some ways my experience was similar to yours, shock, anger and despair. I found it hard to believe someone I loved so much might die and there was nothing I could do, except pray. I did pray and, in the process, I gained a deeper faith in God. I realise meditating has helped me.

"I've also found the last few months really hard both physically and emotionally. I know you're going through a lot and I want to give you time to rest, so I'm doing everything. And that has been exhausting. I haven't stopped since July. I'm hoping in the new year everything will settle down and I'll be able to rest too.

"Do you want to take a vacation before I go back to work next week? We can ask someone look after the children and go to Daylesford for the weekend."

"That would be great," she said as she considered who she could ask to take care of the children.

Daylesford was a tiny country town with natural mineral water springs. It was a quiet place where more and more people were moving in search of an alternative lifestyle. We spent a wonderful weekend there and talked a lot about what we wanted our lives to be like and how we could help one another. It was hard on Sara to go to work, take care of the children and take care of me. On Sunday morning, we went to the market and bought a small statue of a wizard carrying a stone. I thought it would look nice in our lounge room.

After a pleasant, relaxed weekend, I started my four-day work week. Of course, the first week was very tiring but I was doing well. I even enjoyed the work again. Internally, I was anxious about the workload, but on the outside, I was very calm, a fact that was pointed out to me by my colleagues as they walked by my desk. The next few weeks passed by without any drama. I was doing the eye exercises regularly in the evening and occasionally palming, during the day. I wanted to do more, so I approached the local Adult Education Centre and offered to run a vision workshop. The woman at the center liked the idea and agreed to the class and told me she and her daughter would be my first students.

I was looking forward to delivering this workshop and the night before the first session, I lay down on the floor of our lounge room and set my intention to clear my mind by taking slow deep breaths. As I did this, I felt a pain in my stomach and was determined to breathe through it. I breathed deeper and deeper until I no longer felt the pain. Then I noticed my breathing became shallow because I was no longer focusing on my breath but on a bright blue light that surrounded me. I instinctively placed my left hand on my heart and my right hand just below my throat and felt the heat that was being generated by my hands, exactly as it had happened during the Reiki session, several months ago. I stayed in this position for about ten minutes, feeling calm and savouring the time, which felt like hours. I put my hands unconsciously to my eyes in the palming position. The same heat surged through my eyes and over my head. It felt so good I did not want it to stop, but I was unable to maintain the position as my eyes opened and brought me out of the trance and I was back in my lounge room.

I continued to lie on the floor, enjoying the sensation and my thoughts shifted to Jesus. I thought of how he had used his hands to heal the sick. I stood up and went to my bookcase to locate my old copy of the *Good News Bible*. I started reading the Gospel of Mark looking for instances of Jesus healings. This was the first time I read an entire Gospel in one sitting. It was only twenty-nine pages long and I was enthralled with every word. For me, the Bible was always something you quoted when you wanted to reinforce a belief. I had not considered reading this incredible book in full.

Now, I found stories to which I could really relate. Ones, I had not been taught in Sunday school or heard in church. I read the story of Bartimaeus, a blind man, and it resonated with me because it was about vision.

"Many of the people scolded him and told him to be quiet. But he shouted even more loudly, 'Son of David, have mercy on me!' Jesus stopped and said, 'Call him.' So, they called the blind man. 'Cheer up!' they said, 'Get up, he is calling you.' So, he threw off his cloak, jumped up, and came to Jesus. 'What do you want me to do for you?' Jesus asked him. 'Teacher,' the blind man answered, 'I want to see again.' 'Go,' Jesus told him, 'your faith has made you well.' At once he was able to see and followed Jesus on the road."

What was reinforced for me was Jesus could heal in two ways; first, by putting his hands on the sick and second, the person's faith was an important part of the healing process. I understood, at that moment, each of us has the power to heal ourselves. I did not discuss this with anyone but Sara, because I was worried that people would consider me to be odd. I was certain discovering the biblical story and having the revelation occurred so I would continue my journey to heal myself. That night, David had a headache and an upset stomach. He was lying in bed and I sat beside him and asked him to close his eyes. I placed one hand on his stomach and the other on his forehead. "Your hand is warm, Daddy," he said to me.

"Just lie still and ask Jesus to make you better," I whispered as I prayed with him.

A few minutes later he opened his eyes and smiled, "My tummy is not sore any more. Thank you, Daddy." I was surprised and delighted I could help him without any medication. Moments later he was fast asleep.

The phone rang early the next morning, "Hello, this is Mike Opia. May I speak to Joshua, please?"

"Hello Greg," I replied, picking up on the myopia pun. He called to wish me luck with my first workshop. We chatted about my plan to walk in with a cane and a seeing-eye dog. His enthusiasm and support lifted my spirits and confidence. I started the day feeling exhilarated and filled with energy.

The day was a success. I explained some of the

Chapter 5 — A Different Way of Doing

possible reasons for wearing glasses and everyone could recall some trauma they had experienced the year they found their eyesight deteriorate to the point where they had to start wearing glasses. Most of the participants mentioned the loss of a favourite grandparent. For some, it was moving to a new house and leaving people they loved behind. It was a time of instability.

In the afternoon I focused on healing with hands. We spent some time in the yard where I had demonstrated sunning and a few other outdoor vision exercises. One woman explained she could not sit on the ground because she had a bad back. I asked for permission to place my hand on her back. She agreed. As I placed my hand on her back, she could feel the warmth radiating from my hand. I could feel the pain draining from her back and into the ground.

Within minutes, she was pain free and was able to sit down. However, later in the day she became skeptical and said the relief she had felt was in her imagination, and now she was in pain again. When the workshop ended, she left with a vague comment about getting in touch with me, but I knew I wouldn't see her again. She chose not to believe.

I still wasn't sure what I was doing, so I decided not to practice this healing energy on anyone outside of my family. I wanted to learn more about Reiki before I could help others understand its powers. I decided to take the following Tuesday off work, since I was committed to a four-day week, and decided to go to the 'The Silver Tree' bookshop where I had my first life changing meditation experience. It was good for me to take a day off to destress and recharge.

I arrived at 'The Silver Tree' at nine-thirty in the morning with plans to sit in on a meditation session that was starting in an hour. This was not my second visit. I had been dropping in for books on visualisation and meditation. Today, I just wanted to browse and speak with the owner, Emily.

There was one other person in the shop. He was a tall, well-built man with a long, black ponytail. He looked to be in his forties and was browsing through some new age CDs at the back of the room next to an open fireplace. Emily was arranging some books but stopped what she was doing and introduced me to him. His name was Ivan Stevens.

"Hi, nice to meet you, Joshua," Ivan said as he shook my hand. "It's good to see another male in this place. We seem to be outnumbered most of the time." I was aware that women outnumbered men in the meditation workshops. In my vision workshop, only two of the twelve participants were men.

"Maybe men aren't as willing to open themselves up and become vulnerable. What do you think?" We developed a quick rapport and were feeling very comfortable with each other.

"I think that's changing slowly." Ivan said. "We've been conditioned to believe a man's role is to be provider and protector. It probably stems from the cave man days when only the strongest males survived. Now, some men are beginning to be open to expressing their

Chapter 5 — A Different Way of Doing

feelings, they're called S.N.A.G.S."

"What?" I asked, knowing what he was saying was correct.

"S.N.A.G.S.; sensitive new age guys! Being sensitive has nothing to do with your sexual preference. It is about being able to share life experiences and being supportive. Women have always been able to do that."

I felt very relaxed chatting with Ivan. We shared the same challenges of integrating these new ways of thinking into our daily lives. We talked about the confusion around a man's role today and we both wanted to do it all; take complete responsibility and at the same time, expand our views of who we are.

We had both come to the bookstore with plans to attend the meditation session, but we were so involved in our conversation, we missed it. We were leaving the store and had agreed to continue our conversation on another day when Ivan suggested Sara and I come to his house at Buninyong for dinner. We exchanged phone numbers and I said I looked forward to seeing him soon.

On my way out, I picked up a brochure from the counter. It was for a Reiki seminar, for people who wanted to become Reiki channels. It was offered by Martha Brooks, the Reiki channel who had come to my house when I first arrived home from hospital.

After getting home, I rang Martha, who was very pleased to hear from me. "I don't know why," I stated, "but I would like to know more about your Reiki seminar. When are you conducting the training? And how much is it?"

"You called at a good time," she said. "A woman is coming down from Sydney this weekend for an initiation workshop, and you're welcome to join us. The cost is five hundred dollars."

"I'm not sure," I hesitated. "I think it might be too expensive. I'll have to talk to my wife."

Martha ignored my last comment, "If you plan to come for the weekend, please come Friday night for the initiation. Think about whether you're ready or not, the money will take care of itself, if this is what you're meant to do."

Sara and I talked about attending the training session, that night. I explained I felt what I was doing with my hands was important and attending Martha's workshop would be relevant to what was happening for me. On the other hand, I thought five hundred dollars was too much to spend on a two-day workshop.

"If you want to do it, then do it," Sara replied. "Didn't you say, Martha said the money will take care of itself?"

"But I have never spent five hundred dollars on myself," I replied. My earlier conversation with Ivan came to mind. "I have to provide for my family. I can't spend that kind of money on myself!"

Sara had an answer for that too, "don't think of it as spending it on yourself. Think of it as learning something that can help your family and friends.

Perhaps the Universe is testing you to see if this is really important for you."

Sara convinced me to go ahead and on Friday evening, I entered a campsite near Ballan; a small service town about twenty minutes from Melbourne, where Martha was holding her initiation session.

As soon as I arrived, Martha asked for payment. I hesitated, thinking this was inappropriate for someone who claimed to be spiritual. I considered turning back.

"I felt you weren't fully committed," Martha said, "and that's the reason I immediately asked for the money. You haven't yet reconciled your decision between your heart and mind." She was right. Like a cool wind blowing over me, I realised I was meant to be here. "Yes, I belong here. I'm ready to be initiated." I handed over the money so I could open my heart and mind to what I was about to learn. Martha took it and ushered me into a large room.

I could not see very much of the campsite in the dark. I went inside the cottage, took off my shoes, and noticed the walls were lined with natural timber, and decorated with Native American Indian drums and feathers. There was a wooden dining room table in the corner with six multi-coloured cushioned chairs. Over-sized cushions covered the floor. Martha placed one of the chairs in the middle of the room. "Sit down, Joshua and I'll initiate you now and for the next two days you'll learn how to use this gift."

I sat in the chair and closed my eyes. Martha started

One Vision

with a silent prayer and then reached down and put her hand on my feet. I had a sense we were not alone, although I knew we were. Her hands were warm and shortly I felt that mine were too. I was told to focus on my breath and with each breath to repeat the words 'love… compassion... peace'. I heard someone whisper those words to me with each breath.

I saw a strong white light and felt compelled to open my eyes to see if it was coming from outside of the room. I felt safe. Martha was standing behind me and she had her hands on my head. I saw a lit candle in front of me and wondered if that was the white light I was seeing when my eyes were closed. I closed my eyes again, but the light had disappeared though the candle was still right in front of me. Martha then circled a feather around me "to cleanse my aura" she said. "It's complete and we're done for tonight. I will see you at eight o'clock sharp tomorrow."

I left the campsite, not sure what had happened. That night, I dreamed I was in a spaceship made from toy blocks. Star Wars type battles were taking place. When the battles ended, a tune played over and over with the words, 'I have to go home'. I even woke up humming the tune and wrote out the dream on a note pad next to my bed so I could share it with Martha later.

When I arrived back at the campsite the next morning, Martha was waiting for me outside. The site was covered in Australian gum trees and other native plants. I looked out in the distance and noticed two koalas eating their meal before retiring for the day's sleep. There were some fenced areas, probably to keep in the small wallabies that wandered about freely.

Martha was speaking to me as a wallaby jumped in between us and into the bushland. "I look after some of these wallabies for the Ballarat Wildlife Park. They are friendly and you can feed them later if you like. There are two goats, but as much as I enjoy their company, I would prefer a cat or dog."

We went inside the cabin and Martha introduced me to the other participant, Beverly, the woman from Sydney. I went into the kitchen and made a cup of lemongrass tea and brought it back to the main room and sat down on a cushion.

When we were seated, Martha said, "Welcome to what I hope will be a special weekend. I've never worked with a group of only two, so it will be an interesting experience for me too. Let me give you some background information about the history of Reiki. Reiki is a Japanese word that means universal life energy; energy surrounds us and is in constant motion. It is there and everyone can tap into it. Its healing motion triggers the body's ability to bring about balance in every area of your life; physical, emotional, intellectual and spiritual.

"Reiki was started in the late eighteen hundreds by Dr. Mikao Usui, a Japanese theologian. He spent many years researching and studying the religions and ancient writings of Japan, India, Tibet and China, in his quest to learn how great beings were able to heal the sick. He then went to Koriyama, a holy mountain in Japan, and fasted and meditated for twenty-one days.

One Vision

"During that time, he had a mystical vision of the workings of Reiki and he spent the rest of his life teaching others this powerful source. When Reiki is activated, your hands become hot and you can feel the energy moving through you. It is not coming from you; it flows from the universe and you are the channel which it passes through.

"Reiki boosts the body's immune system and, in the process speeds up healing. It cannot replace medical treatment, but it can enhance it. Many health professionals incorporate Reiki into their practice."

I was intending to use Reiki on myself, my family and possibly a few friends. It did not even occur to me to offer it to anyone else, especially clients. Martha explained she would teach us both Reiki One and Two so by the end of the weekend we would know the complete system.

She told us Reiki uses a number of healing symbols, the primary one is a heart shaped symbol called 'Mai Yur Ma' pronounced 'My-you-a-ma'. It represents the heart and unconditional love. It contains three infinity symbols inside the heart. The eight is the symbol of infinity, and represents the infinite power of love and ends at the heart chakra.

Then we learned symbols for grounding, so the Reike session did not exhaust the person, but instead left him or her feeling peaceful. There was a symbol for protection too, that dispels any negative energy present.

On the second day, we learned how to place our

Chapter 5 A Different Way of Doing

hands while applying Reiki. "You have the person lying on a table or sitting in a chair. I will teach you form. You can decide how to apply it. You can place your hand anywhere as long as you get the client's permission.

I was feeling like I was home. I felt more love for myself and confidence in my ability. I was becoming less judgmental. My life had taken a turn and I was on a different path. I no longer needed a tumour to help me evolve. I could continue my journey without the fear of another operation should I occasionally stray from my life's purpose.

At the end of the weekend, Martha handed me a piece of paper. It was a note she had written right after my initiation on Friday night. I sat on a cushion and read, '*Joshua, when I put my hands on you, Dr. Usui and others were there to welcome you. We did a great deal of work around your head hemispheres, third eye and crown chakras. We used a lot of purple and forest green colours. You will be an inspiration to many. These are only you first steps. Go with the flow and be discerning when you choose your teachers. A lot will open up for you in time, so be patient and it will come. In love and trust. Martha.*'

We hugged and said our good-byes, and I went home, certain this weekend would have an impact on my family and me. I did a healing session on Sara. She could feel the energy throughout the house as it worked through her. She even commented the light tapping sound we heard coming from the kitchen may be spirits giving their approval.

The next morning, a cheque from Sara's parents arrived in the mail. They said it was paid to us from a trust that Sara didn't know about. The Universe had indeed provided, and the cost of the Reiki course was repaid. The learning for me was that I had passed a test regarding the feeling of financial scarcity. There is abundancy in the world. At work the next day, I told the story to a colleague whom I felt would appreciate the link. He did not. He said he could not see a correlation between the two events and dismissed it as just a coincidence. I stopped sharing my experiences because people at work just did not seem to understand, and I was worried they might judge me to be flawed. Sara and the children were accepting and supportive. Sara even suggested she might be interested in learning Reiki. I was grateful to have a family that was open to change and to personal growth. This helped me cope with the dejection I felt at work. I started to feel I would be happier in some other profession.

A week after I completed the Reiki course, I received a phone call from a woman who introduced herself as Jillian Parker. "Greg told me about you," she said. "I've been working on improving my vision. Greg told me you've done an amazing job with yours."

"I'm still working on it," I told her, "but I'm now able to drive without wearing glasses." She was excited and asked if she could meet me. "Greg mentioned you also do Reiki."

"Well, yes." I answered.

"Can I please make an appointment for a session this

week?" Jillian asked enthusiastically.

"Of course!" I was surprised and excited I was actually getting my first client. Jill came over to the house a few days later and I gave my first Reiki session to a person outside of my family. Even though I was nervous to begin with, the session was successful, and she told me she would tell all her friends. I was pleased with myself, but I knew I needed more training, so I phoned Michelle.

She had mentioned Chiron Healing to me, during my chiropractic session and I had dismissed it at the time, but now I knew I should explore it. I asked her when she was teaching the Chiron Healing class again and booked myself into the workshop in three weeks' time. The cost was only ninety dollars.

Prior to the workshop, I went back to Greg for another vision test. He told me the tumour was still there but did not seem to be affecting my sight. The improvements with my vision were noteworthy and I would not need to see him again until the end of the year.

I was now meditating every night alone or with Sara. For a few days before the Chiron Healing workshop, I was meditating just before I went to bed. This evening, I drifted off to sleep with a sensation my body was being overcome by someone or something. A male voice called my name and I woke up suddenly. I called out to Sara, "did you hear that?" as I sat up. Sara did not move but replied cautiously, "I think it's your guide making himself known."

"What's a guide?" I asked, sounding scared.

"A guide is from the spirit world. It is their job is to be of service to you," she said. Sara had grown so much since she had joined me in my exploration of alternate healing. "He's here to support your knowledge of trance mediumship."

"What's that?" I asked.

"I don't know. It just came to me. You should look into it." I felt relieved and now I was more pleased than worried, and I drifted off into a deep sleep.

I went to Michelle's clinic early the next morning. We were seated in an old Victorian style room; the cornices and skirting boards painted shades of pale lilac. It felt peaceful. Michelle introduced the workshop leaders, Rosemary and Jane to the five participants. Then she took her seat as a participant too.

"Welcome," Rosemary began. "The purpose of this weekend is to introduce you to the foundations of Chiron Healing and new and practical ways of healing. I'd like to start with a prayer, so I'd like to know if there is anyone here who isn't Christian." We all responded that we were. She recited the Lord's Prayer, and the group followed.

She went to a whiteboard and drew an outline of a body and pointed to the various auras and their location. "You can work on any level, sometimes you'll use your intuition and sometimes muscle testing."

She described the muscle test similar to what I had

experienced at the Alternative Festival. She talked about how to test the balance in the three main lines of energy. The centre line governed the balance between the left and right sides of the body and ran through the entire body. The right represented the Yang or masculine side and would constitute the physical ailments. The left side was the Yin or feminine side and controlled the spiritual states.

Rosemary explained healing is done by clearing and protecting the body's energy. "We have our own energy and we pick up the energies of others in the same way as we pick up germs. Some of that energy is positive and creates love, and others are negative and create anger and fear, among other emotions. We don't label either as good or bad. They just are.

"When you feel you've experienced negative energy, I clear it by saying something like, 'I clear all negative energy and bind it up to the white light'. This will protect you from the energy and prevent it from coming back at any time. I might follow up with something like; 'I clothe myself in a robe of white light composed of the love, power and wisdom of God'. By doing this, I guarantee my energy is not depleted while I work with someone else. White light is a sign of God. I also wear at least one article of white clothing when I'm working."

I was comforted by the thought of all this energy coming from God, rather than speaking of it as a universal energy. Although the words you use to describe love and fear are not important, I could relate to God more since I grew up in a religious home.

One Vision

We learned various methods of etheric levels including a comprehensive series of triangles and diamonds that covered the body.

Rosemary described how to use our name to examine our life's lessons. "Apply a number to each letter in your name. One for A, J and S, Two for B, K and T, three for C, L and U, four for D, M and V, five for E, N and W, six for F, G, O, P, X and Y and seven for H, I, Q, R and Z. For example, Joshua would have three lots of one for the J, S and A, one lot of three for the U, one lot of six for the O and one seven for the H."

I wrote out my name, Joshua Clark Winter, to apply Rosemary's numbering system to the letters. My name consisted of four letters for the number one, three for two, two for three, none for four, three for five, one for six and three for the number seven. Rosemary continued to explain how the groups of numbers gave insights into our life's lessons. "The number with the smallest total overall is what you have come into this world to work on or, if you like, your lesson in this life. If your name has more letters in any one grouping than the others, this may indicate that you may have an over-abundance of a particular quality associated with the life lesson."

Rosemary resumed by describing each of the life lessons connected to the numbers from one through to seven. "If you have none or very few letters scoring the number one, then your lesson in life would be to care more for others. If two, then your lesson would relate to caring for yourself. I find this number comes up a lot with health practitioners, who are always giving and rarely taking time for themselves. For the number three, your lesson would be to practice sitting in quiet contemplation, without resentment. Four would be sharing all of your accumulated knowledge with others."

I thought for a moment about the life lesson for the number four as I did not have any letters in that group. According to Rosemary, this would be the area I need to look at in this life, although I was still unclear what she meant by this life.

"Five is the feeling line. Your lesson here would be to show empathy for what others are feeling. The lesson of the number six relates to gaining strength by helping others on their path. If you have only a few letters in the seventh group, then your lesson is to avoid getting stuck in day to day problems but rather look at the big picture."

The last lesson on the first day was about chakras, which I already had some knowledge about. "Chakras are the main energy centres in the body. There are seven centres, and each is associated with a colour. The first is referred to as the base chakra and is located in the genital area and is associated with physical attributes and the colour red. The second chakra is located just below the navel and expresses emotions. It is normally orange. The third is located around the stomach and refers to the intellect and is associated with the colour yellow. The fourth chakra is located in the heart area and refers to balance and is associated with the colour green. The fifth chakra, which is located in the neck, refers to healing and the colour blue. The sixth chakra is near the pituitary and is also referred to as the third eye and associated with the colour indigo and deals with intuition. The final chakra is in the upper portion of the head and refers to everything spiritual and is associated with the colours violet or white."

We started the next day with another prayer, and Rosemary continued her lecture on chakras. "Yesterday I told you about the chakras and the various colours that are normally associated with them. However, that is not exactly correct. Those colours are not always the same. Let us explore what I mean by meditating and each of you focus on each of the chakras to see what colours appear to you." As I began my meditation, I recalled the colours in Greg's colour machine. I started to focus on each of my chakras. I was surprised to see the colours were different from the ones Rosemary had described. I saw my first chakra as green brown; the second was brown orange; the third a yellow-gold; the fourth a light green; the fifth a dark blue, the sixth was purple and the seventh was white but with a yellow circle in the center. It was a fascinating experience. The range of colours were exhilarating.

We spent the rest of the morning going over what we learned and were introduced to a few more healing techniques. I was beginning to understand how the triangles and diamonds were used.

Jane took over from Rosemary for the afternoon session. She sat in the chair at the front of the room and introduced herself.

"I'm going to ask Chira to come through me. I only allow myself to be used as a channel when it is for a higher good. Teaching a new group of enlightened students is one of those times." This was my first experience seeing someone channel a spirit and I was a little skeptical. Jane closed her eyes and began some very deep breathing.

A few minutes later she was speaking in a different voice. "Welcome, my friends," she said with a slight Asian accent, "my name is Chira. I am pleased to see so many of you here today. There are a few things I wish to tell you." The room was still, our attention fixed on Jane.

I closed my eyes so nothing would distract me from hearing what Chira was saying. Chira continued, "Everyone should spend regular time in quiet contemplation. How you do that is up to you. If you do not have a private space, do it anywhere you can be alone and quiet. It is only when you do that will you find the answers are already in you. You will not find them from others.

"Believe there are no coincidences in the spirit plane. Everything happens for a reason, be it a person who comes into your life or the occurrence of an event. A child's arm breaks, there is a lesson in that. He will be more careful while climbing a tree."

I thought about each person I had met lately. Each one seemed to turn up at exactly the right time. Each taught me something or led me along a different path. Perhaps, I had also turned up at the right time for them. Chira expanded on these points and then she gave each of us a personal message. I was the first to whom Chira

One Vision

spoke. "To the gentleman in the corner, you will be working with people who believe they are terminally ill but only about one percent of them actually are. For the others, it is only in their imagination. Do you understand?"

I opened my eyes to see the others nod in agreement. I was an accountant. What did Chira mean? "No," I murmured. "Could you please explain it?" Chira simply repeated the same message and asked, "Is it clearer?" It was not but I did not want to appear confused. I was so focused on trying to understand her message to me, I did not hear what was said to the others.

At the end of the day, when we were all leaving, I went over to Michelle and asked her to interpret for me what Chira's message meant. She smiled and replied, "You'll find out, Joshua. You'll find out."

In Dreams

The week before Easter I answered a call from Ivan. We talked with our wives and arranged to have dinner at their home on Thursday evening. We organised for the children to stay overnight with their friends as Ivan's children were going to be with their grandparents until Easter Sunday.

Bunninyong is a very small country town about fifteen kilometers from Ballarat. Like Ballarat, it was built during the gold rush and had not grown very much since.

However, as Sara and I drove into the town of Bunninyong, I noticed some positive changes. There were several new buildings and the streets were becoming stylish in their appearance. The new buildings were large, single story, brick veneer houses, reflecting those of the town built in the early 1920's.

One Vision

We followed Ivan's clear directions and found his home on a hill at the end of the town. In contrast to the houses we had passed, his new home had two stories. The ground floor was constructed of dark clay bricks and the top floor was made of treated cedar boards. Ivan had said on the phone that the house was finished but the verandah had not yet been built. "Welcome," Ivan greeted us as we walked up the path, "I'd like you to meet my wife, Magda." Magda was much shorter than Ivan and had a slight European accent.

I said hello and then introduced them both to Sara. As we entered the house, Magda brought out some apple cider and offered us a drink. Coincidentally, it was the same as the bottle I brought to give to them for hosting us and it made us laugh which broke the ice.

We were sitting in the lounge room and I noticed they did not have a television. The walls were bare except for a few spotlights that effectively lit the room. Below one of these spotlights there was a narrow, hall table covered by coloured stones. "I'm admiring the stones on your table," I commented, mostly to start up a conversation.

"They're crystals," Magda explained, "Pick one up and hold it in your hand."

I picked up a small piece of a purple coloured quartz crystal, and as I closed my palm over the crystal, I felt a tingling sensation. "My hand feels like it's vibrating," I said surprised.

"That crystal is an amethyst," said Magda. "It's great

for meditation and to relieve stress."

"How do crystals work?" I asked, quite interested in what she was saying.

"Crystals store energy, much like a battery stores electricity. They make silicon chips for computers from the crystalline in silica. The quartz crystal is a conductor of subtle energy which it releases when you hold it in your hand."

I was fascinated by it and gave it to Sara to hold as I picked up a few more crystals. I noticed the tingling feeling from each piece of crystal varied. When I picked up a piece of clear quartz with black streaks through it, I could feel the general tiredness I had been experiencing for a few weeks dissipate. I felt rejuvenated.

Magda was explaining each piece as I picked it up. "That is a rutilated quartz. It works on the pituitary and is great for cuts and abrasions."

I remarked the rutilated quartz had a tangible effect on me; I felt renewed. I described my operation and added I had been feeling very tired, pushing myself to get everything finished. But now I was amazed at how I was feeling. Magda was very pleased and told me the piece must have been meant for me and to accept it as a gift from her.

Ivan served us a delicious vegetarian dinner. Before the meal, we held hands and Ivan blessed the food and gave thanks for our new friendship. We were relaxed and felt safe in each other's company. Magda talked about having been a vegetarian for several years but

One Vision

added that she was starting to include some meat in her diet, lately. I explained we had started to reduce the amount of meat we ate as well, especially red meat. "We do eat other animal proteins but in smaller amounts and fewer times in a week."

"We don't eat pork, with the exception of some well-cooked bacon," Ivan interjected. "We follow Edgar Cayce on these matters."

"Who is that?" I asked.

"Edgar Cayce. He gave readings under self-hypnosis on topics such as nutrition, health, and dreams. In one of his readings he says the only pork one should eat is well-cooked bacon and even that, sparingly."

We ate our meal and enjoyed a friendly conversation with our hosts, and not much more was said about Cayce. After dinner, we retired to the lounge room and I picked up the subject, "Ivan, please tell me more about Edgar Cayce?" I asked because something about the man interested me.

"You're asking about one of my favourite subjects and I'll try not to bore you." Ivan smiled as he started. "Edgar Cayce was born in Kentucky, U.S.A. in 1877 and died in 1945. He was very religious and taught Sunday school. He first read the Bible, in its entirety, when he was young, and he made a point of reading it, once a year. He had some difficulties at school, until he fell asleep, one night, while doing his homework. He put his schoolbook under his pillow and when he woke up the next morning, he could fully recall the contents of

Chapter 6 — In Dreams

the book. His Presbyterian upbringing wouldn't allow him to use this new talent.

"Years later, when he was married, he developed a throat irritation and he lost his voice. The doctors could not find an answer and were unable do anything for him. He decided to see a local hypnotist. Under hypnosis, Cayce was able to speak, and he also diagnosed his own illness and recommend the treatment that cured him.

"Later, he discovered he could do the same for others. In a hypnotic state, he diagnosed illnesses and recommend treatments with astonishing accuracy. He had no knowledge of anatomy or physiology in his waking state. Often, he did not know the name of the health practitioners he directed people to or the herbs he recommended. However, when he stopped this practice in response to public reaction, he lost his voice again until he resumed the readings. He decided this was a gift and it was what God wanted him to do." Ivan was very animated as he spoke about this man.

Fascinated by the story, I asked, "Were his readings always health related?"

"No, he soon realised once under self-hypnosis, Cayce could answer questions on any subject. At first, people were sending him only medical questions, and these were from all over the country. He did not remember anything he said while in a trance, so he had a stenographer write everything down. Later, he was getting questions on all sorts of topics and he was able to respond to those too. His mind had a vast universal store of knowledge that became known as the Akashic

One Vision

Records. These life readings included dreams and meditations.

"Study groups started to form for the sole purpose of studying the readings because everything had been recorded. A group, known as the Association for Research and Enlightenment or the A. R. E., is dedicated to learning from the fifteen thousand readings Cayce gave during his life. The A.R.E. is based in Virginia Beach, where Cayce lived at the end of his life. It organises conferences on Cayce's work and is committed to helping people realise their true relationship to themselves, the world, and with God.

"The A.R.E. have classified the readings into various topics. The readings about physical ailments cover hundreds of illnesses from the common cold, allergies, to treatments for cancer. Suggested treatments have been found to be incredibly effective. He also did readings on matters concerning the origin and destiny of man, karma, reincarnation, Atlantis, ESP and the life and works of Christ. His readings were very much influenced by his love of Jesus, whom he refers to as 'The Master'."

"How is it that you know so much about him?" Sara asked, fascinated by what she was hearing.

"I have studied Cayce for years and have read most of the books by him and about him. I would be happy to give you a copy of a book about his life. I think you will find it very interesting.

We talked for some time and shared much about

ourselves, and before the evening came to an end, we made plans to get together after lunch on Easter Sunday with the children, so they could also get to know each other.

Sara and I were happy to have made new friends. We had enjoyed the evening spent with Ivan and Magda. Ivan was very knowledgeable about New Age ideas and therapies. I was looking forward to reading about Edgar Cayce and seeing them again on Sunday.

I could relate to Edgar Cayce's struggle, reconciling his gifts with the church's teachings. So often I felt just like he did, doubting myself and my abilities. Ivan had said he often felt like giving up to focus on his photography business. Time and again, as he tried to bring a group of people together to demonstrate his psychic readings, things would turn out badly. It was only after he surrendered himself to God things started to go well. He had been drawn to Virginia Beach, which had a small population at the time. He had been able to buy a reasonably priced house and because of him, the town become a major tourist attraction and headquarters for A.R.E.

The children woke up early on Easter Sunday to discover Easter eggs at the bottom of their beds. They ran downstairs to show them to Sara and me. We pretended to be sleepy, all the while trying hard to stop ourselves from laughing and revealing our secret. We sent them to the den to watch television. While Sara went to organise breakfast, I managed to go back to sleep and had a two-part dream.

One Vision

In the first part of my dream, I had been at a library to do some research and when I went back to my car, I found a parking ticket on the windshield. I actually felt the emotion of being annoyed. As I looked around, I saw a bicycle. Then the scene changed. I saw myself in heaven baking scones for a group of about twelve people. With that I woke up.

Sitting up in bed, I remembered what Ivan had said about Edgar Cayce and his ability to explain dreams, so I quickly wrote my dreams down to discuss them with Ivan, later. I was hoping he might be able to tell me what they meant. I had been starting to believe more and more that my dreams would help me to get in touch with myself. Meditating was no longer helping me. I was able to guide my meditations but not my dreams.

My father joined us for lunch, and I found our ability to hold a conversation was so much better than it had been for a long time. I asked him about my youth hoping he might have some insights into where I was heading. His recollection about my childhood was so different from mine. We seemed to remember the same events but our views of them were often the opposite. I found it interesting how differently people see things.

After my father left, we went to meet Ivan and Magda at their home. Magda introduce their children to us. Jeremy was twelve, Alana, seven and Christopher, four. David and Jeremy went off together happily, but it took Alana a few minutes to convince our shy Melissa, to come and play with Christopher and her.

After we saw the children enjoying each other's

Chapter 6 *In Dreams*

company, we sat down to some tea and biscuits. I told Ivan I had finished reading the Edgar Cayce book he had lent me, and he beamed and asked me what I thought about it.

"I liked the fact he was just an ordinary person until he was about thirty-four. I could relate to and admire him and his passion to help people. I was fascinated by the fact the miracles from the Bible could happen today too." Then I told Ivan about my dream. Sometimes I could interpret my dreams, but I had found this one was confusing. Ivan listened to me finish before he spoke.

"A library generally means knowledge which is why you were there, and probably relates to all the learning you've been doing these days. The parking ticket annoyed you. Cars in dreams may mean the physical body. Getting a parking ticket could be interpreted as a warning you are moving too fast. The bike might suggest you need to create more balance.

"As for baking twelve scones in heaven; Edgar Cayce might see that as a good sign. The twelve people in heaven may be the twelve apostles. I interpret this is a message you too can achieve your purpose, just like the apostles, by maintaining a balance in your life. What do you think? Does this make sense to you?"

"Absolutely! I find most days, I am unbalanced. Some days, I am filled with energy and on other days, I just want to sleep. I think the dream is also telling me I need to rely on myself more and less on others."

"That's a good point," Ivan replied, "but there are

times when I am also overwhelmed and need a kick start from someone, and that person is often Magda. She uses kinesiology to locate emotional blocks of which I'm not even aware."

"It sounds very much like the Chiron healing I learned recently. Anyway, getting back to dreams, what are some things Cayce said about dreams?" I asked, anxious to know more about this man.

"Cayce saw dreams as a way for your subconscious or higher self to connect to your conscious mind. When we are awake, we often obstruct our highest good with our minds, wishing for something different. Dreams help raise our self-awareness by linking our conscious and subconscious mind.

"Some dreams are more important than others. For example, if you wake up from a dream in the middle of the night, you should write it down, so you won't forget it by the morning. Others may be the ones you have repeatedly or are in colour. In some cultures, dreams that occur on major dates like birthdays or New Year's Day tend to be more significant.

"It's very hard to remember all the details in your dreams, so it's very useful to use a dream journal and write down the aspects of the dream and any feelings you can recall. You can also prepare yourself to recall your dreams by not eating too much, drinking coffee, or watching television before bed. This could mean you don't get a good night's sleep, and it can also interfere in the dream process.

"You need to have a positive attitude to get clarity from your dreams. Cayce suggested if your waking state is a mess, you also cannot expect clarity in your dreams. He also said you are the best interpreter of your dreams. That's why I might say something like a car represents the physical body. But if you're a car salesman, it represents work. Ultimately, each person should decide what the dream is saying to them.

"That does not mean you shouldn't use books on dreams or get guidance from others. In my experience, I find dreams reflect whatever resources the dreamer can access. It's uncanny how often someone will tell me their dreams contain so many of the symbols they see in the day to day. Be careful with the books you buy to help interpret your dreams because many will tell you elements in your dreams are about sex or wealth and they are not.

"Having said that, Cayce saw certain things could be generally interpreted, such as a car headlight or windows of a house could relate to your eyesight or your inner vision. After all, your eyes are the windows to the soul. The dream may mean there is something you need to look at or it might mean something is physically wrong with your eyes. You would have to consider the rest of the dream for a broader explanation.

"To interpret symbols in your dreams, write them down and then look up what they might represent in a book, before applying it to yourself. For example, a policeman will likely represent an authority figure; someone dying may represent the death of an idea or a viewpoint. As I said before, Cayce felt that feelings, like fear, anger or love, associated with a dream gave you a fuller picture.

"Another interesting aspect of dreams I have been exploring lately is setting an intent before falling asleep. As I'm going to sleep, I might think of something that's concerning me that I would like to resolve and when I do that, I'll actually dream about it. The dream doesn't necessarily provide me with an answer, but it might enlighten me to the issues. I often spend a long time writing down a dream because there are so many details coming through it."

Sara and Magda brought us some peppermint tea. "Ivan has been explaining dreams to me," I told them, before turning my attention back to Ivan.

"The benefit of analysing your dreams," continued Ivan, "is to expand your consciousness and to develop spiritually. The things that present themselves to us in our dreams can guide us through health and personal challenges. People gain guidance for business matters; they find encouragement and inspiration."

"What about when a dream is lucid?" Sara asked, joining the conversation.

"A lucid dream is when you consciously know you are dreaming and can change the content of the dream. For example, if you are aware you are falling, Cayce would suggest you put a pillow down to break your fall. I used to think this type of dream was interrupting some subconscious thought that was being activated by in the dream. But now, I think your higher self is letting you know you can choose how to handle the situation."

"The type of dream I like best is when I'm shown something or hear a specific phrase repeated. One example was when I dreamed that Cayce was handing me an Olympic torch. The message to me was I should be following in Cayce's footsteps and continue his work. That is the main reason I am so engaged in learning as much as I can about Cayce's work."

Magda had been sitting quietly and now joined in. "I have a dream catcher above my bed and believe it helps me remember my dreams. I also have a piece of amethyst beside my bed. Crystals have immense powers for so many things, and this is just one," she said as her face lit up with a smile.

We heard one of the children fall and our conversation suddenly ended. Alana came running in crying. She had fallen and hurt her knee. Magda didn't appear to be overly concerned. She put one hand on Alana's knee and the other on her forehead. In less than a minute, Alana had stopped crying although she was still shaken by the incident. Magda put Alana on the couch and went to the kitchen. She came back carrying a small bottle with a dropper and put two drops under Alana's tongue. "This is called Rescue Remedy," Magda explained, "It helps reduce shock."

Alana soon relaxed. Magda, then, went back into the kitchen and brought us all bowls of fried rice for dinner. While we ate, I asked Magda if she could show me how her approach to kinesiology worked. I suggested I would do some energy work on Ivan if Magda would do a session with me. I felt comfortable offering to do energy work on Ivan because then I could see if what I did for myself would work on others.

Magda and I went into another room where she asked me to lie down on a massage table. She asked me then, how I had been feeling lately. I explained I was seeing good results from meditation and it was helping to reduce the side-effects of the surgery. "When did you have the operation?" Magda enquired.

"About ten months ago," I replied, "but I'm not fully recovered from it yet. Sometimes I wonder if there was any benefit to removing the tumour."

"I think you're pushing yourself too much. You need to take it easy," Magda said, feeling the tension in my body as she did some muscle testing. "I tend to work on a person's emotional side more than using applied kinesiology," she said as she tested my left arm, "this releases blockage that are stopping personal development. I am now feeling some sort of issue from your childhood. Is there anything that comes to mind right now?"

"That's interesting. I had just thought about the time I was thirteen and started shaving. My family laughed at me and humiliated me instead of helping me by giving me instructions on how do it correctly. I felt so embarrassed." Magda stopped what she was doing and told me to sit up as she handed me a glass of water.

"Have you told the people you work with that you're doing Reiki and Chiron?" Magda asked.

"No, I haven't told them. I don't know if they would understand what it is or if they would find it strange. They would just blame my illness." I said sheepishly.

"Why should it matter to you how people think? It's their problem not yours." Magda replied, in a tough, but understanding tone.

Of course, she was right. I had just as much right to my own beliefs as they did theirs, but it wasn't something that came naturally to me. I worried about what people thought. After a few more adjustments, Magda ended the session which she explained was intended to release emotional blockages around humiliation.

I thanked Magda, and we rejoined Sara and Ivan. Sara was talking about a playing card she had just turned over. "These are Angel cards, Joshua," Sara explained. "They're very accurate in pointing ideas out. Try them."

I was already very pleased about how much I had learned about Edgar Cayce. I wondered how all of this was affecting my life. I sat down and asked Magda to select three cards. The first card was 'Education'. Certainly, I was focused on expanding my mind by constantly reading and learning. The second card was 'Patience', which told me to follow Magda's advice and slow down. The last card was 'Power'. I knew power was something I feared for myself and for others because it was often abused. It was clear there was a message for me in all three cards about aspects of my life I needed to face.

One Vision

It was getting late when we finally managed to coax the children to finish their games and get into the car. As we were saying our good-byes, Ivan told me he had just joined the meditation sessions at The Silver Tree on Thursday nights, and he wondered if I would be interested in going along with him. "It might help encourage more men to attend" he laughed, as I started the car. We waved good night to our hosts as we drove off. It had been a wonderful day for all of us. Sara and I had learned a lot and Ivan and Magda had been so pleased to be able to share their wisdom with us.

I meditated before going to bed and suddenly felt a need to read a Bible passage from the Gospel of Luke. I rarely knew where I would begin to read when I picked up the Bible. Given that so many things were happening to me, that were out of the ordinary, I did not think knowing exactly which passage I wanted to read was unusual. I wrote the reference down, Luke 5: 7-12, so I would remember to look it up in the morning. When I read the Bible in the morning, I recognised the story of the calling of the apostles. The message I took from this was that I was being called to do more.

I decided to join Ivan at the Thursday night meditation. There were several people present whom I had met during the last ten months. Emily, the owner of the shop, and Kate, the facilitator of the first session I had attended, were there too.

In his guided meditation session, Ivan had us traveling through time. I chose to ask a time traveler some questions about his experiences. Each time he answered my questions by saying, no, I felt my elbow

Chapter 6 *In Dreams*

lock. When the session ended and most of the participants had left, I mentioned this to Kate. She found it amusing.

"That's an interesting indicator if I'm correct. Your task is to accept it and use your intuition to find your own answers," Kate said.

"How can I develop my intuition?" I asked.

"Trust yourself. That's it, just trust in yourself. I started with Tarot cards but now I can see my intuition is just as good at guiding me. Of course, I have other guides in my life. By the way, I see you moving from your house in about eight weeks."

"Definitely not!" I said, denying the possibility. "Sara and I were just talking about putting an extension on our house but decided we can't pay for it just yet. So, we certainly can't afford to move either."

"The message came to me, so just keep it in mind."

When I arrived home, I told Sara about my experience and Kate's comments. She also did not see the possibility of moving to a new house. She thought the locked elbow was very interesting. I thought I'd test what happened during the meditation to locate a pair of nail clippers.

I went into the bedroom and immediately my elbow twitched and locked. I went to the children's bathroom and my elbow stayed flexible. I opened the cupboard and my elbow locked. When I touched the bottom shelf, my elbow locked. As I held onto Sara's old toiletry bag my elbow didn't lock, but the nail clippers I found were not mine. I had to be clearer when setting my intent.

I tried this process again and found a missing book under a pile of papers on the dining room table. When I went to try again with someone else in the room, it did not work at all. It seemed I had to be alone when I set my intent, trusting my quest was honest and not a game. I should not abuse a gift. Like Kate said, I had to trust my intuition.

I went back to see Greg at the end of April. My eyesight had improved a lot, but it was not yet twenty-twenty. I told him I was very pleased about what I was learning and offered to do some energy work with him. He said he did not want anyone in Ballarat to treat him and politely declined my offer. I was disappointed but I could understand he was the doctor and I was a patient. But it had been Greg who said healing can occur without a doctor-patient relationship. He still needed to believe it.

I went home still feeling deflated and took out my copy of the Edgar Cayce book and looked up all the references on vision. What I read was very informative and I was encouraged to organise another vision workshop at the community centre. I found references about what to eat to improve eyesight. For example, Cayce recommended carrots, green peas and beans, onions, and beets. He said these vegetables had a direct influence on the optic forces. He suggested applying eye poultices made from a weak Glyco-Thymoline solution poured over grated organic potato. He also mentioned palming fifty years before it became widely known.

Chapter 6 — *In Dreams*

Cayce proposed a twenty-minute walk, and some easy head and neck exercises every day for at least six months were two of the best practices to improve vision. The head and neck exercise were done sitting erect, bending your head forward three times, back three times, to the right side three times, to the left three times, and then to circle your head three times. He said to do these slowly, every day, in good and bad weather. Since it often rains in Ballarat, I was concerned about walking outdoors every day, but I started doing the head and neck exercises. These exercises felt good and seemed to be working.

The adult education centre had gifted me a weekend for two at a local health spa that had some excellent masseuses, so a couple of weeks later, Sara and I decided to take advantage of it, and I made reservations. We enjoyed a wonderful weekend and it gave me some more ideas for integrating a variety of modalities into my seminar.

Sara was beginning to enjoy doing more of these activities with me, especially the massages which we were taught to do on each other. She enjoyed giving a massage but said she would not want to work on anyone but me. She was also becoming interested in Reiki and was ready to book a session for that too. We were enjoying this extra time together and practicing what we had been taught brought us so much closer. When we learned the children could be enrolled in Reiki One, we all became Reiki channels. Melissa was very good at going through the steps and David could put me to sleep.

One evening, Sara had just finished a Reiki treatment on me, and as I lay on the floor in a slightly altered state, I felt my body become lighter until I could hardly feel it touching the floor. In that light state I felt as if I was outside my body drifting around the room. I did not want the peaceful feeling to end. Slowly I felt drawn back inside the figure lying there. I opened my eyes, still in a daze, and felt the heaviness of my body. I realised Sara had left the room but as I looked around there appeared to be a silhouette in the shape of man in the room with me. He looked very happy. The silhouette suddenly disappeared, as Sara came back into the room. I didn't mention what I had seen to Sara, convinced that I had just imagined it.

The next time I saw Michelle Heart I told her. I explained I had been very calm at the time but was less so now when I looked back on the experience. I also revealed there had been another time when I had heard a voice.

Michelle did a Chiron healing, and suggested I say the affirmation, 'I always follow the guidance of my higher self.' She explained these were all learning experiences for me and recommended in order to gain a better understanding of what was happening to me, I should join a Chiron healing circle. "I will join a circle at some point in my journey, but not yet," I told her.

That night, I meditated on these new experiences. I recalled being in the operating room among all the green plants. I had not thought of that scene for a long time and recognised I had had the same feeling then as I did when I was floating outside my body. Going back to the

Chapter 6 *In Dreams*

operating room, I could see the doctors below working on my body and I heard myself talking to them from above. I heard a different voice saying I should go back because I had an important role to play in the future. Now I could actually remember hearing a voice, but I had forgotten it when I woke up after the surgery. As I came out of the meditation trance I wondered, did I die that day on the operating table?

I thought about asking the surgeon if that had been a possibility but decided it didn't really matter now and kept my concerns to myself. I would focus on the work I was doing to improve my eyesight and I looked forward to the two vision workshops Greg was organising. One was going to be led by Victor Capper, the author of the book Greg lent me, when I first started on improving my eyesight. The other was with the American, Andrew Whitecross, who was - returning to Australia.

David was going to a friend's birthday party on the outskirts of Ballarat, so I dropped him off and drove back to Ballarat for a game of squash with an old school friend, John. He had just started a new job with a real estate firm and had suggested I join him for a game. He needed to take a break. I mentioned to John that I really liked the area where David's friend's family lived. He caught me off guard, when he said, "Have I got just the house for you!"

I laughed it off and told him to stop playing his real estate game with me, but he wouldn't take no for an answer. He insisted I take a look. I suggested we make a bet on the outcome of the game, whether I did or did not. If I lost, I would go and see the house. He won all

One Vision

three games.

The house was a large brick veneer home with an area of over twenty-five squares sitting on twelve acres. It had two large living areas and I could already envision how Sara and I could set up one of them as a healing area. The yard was a mess and the décor were awful, but the price was reasonable. It simply needed some cosmetic work. I told John I would bring Sara back to see it when I collected David. When Sara saw the property, she loved it immediately. She had grown up on a farm and valued the extra space. She insisted it would be great for the children and there was so much we could do with a property like this one. We weighed the pros and cons and a week later signed the papers. It was exactly eight weeks and a day since Kate had said we would be moving to a new house.

Our contract was conditional on the sale of our house, which hadn't sold yet. When I contemplated on the date and value of the house, my elbow twitched at end of June for exactly seventy-three thousand dollars. The sale went through on the last day of June for that exact amount, despite my working hard for another five hundred dollars.

In the end, I trusted, and everything worked out well. I could only trust. Both Sara and I knew we must care for the land and we immediately began planting more trees and flowers in the yard. We felt the journey we were on culminated in this ideal home and the road was open to possibilities.

Inner Reflections

Sara and I were celebrating the sale of our house when I took a call from Kate. She had been to see Greg for an eye test. Her eyesight was deteriorating so Greg had suggested she should talk to me about how she could improve it.

"How much do you charge for a consultation?" she asked.

"I don't know," I said, "I've not yet considered working with individuals. What do you think?"

"Let's do a swap," Kate suggested. "I'll give you a reading in exchange for a consultation. If you think that would be fair."

"That sounds reasonable. I'm available this afternoon if that is convenient for you. Come by the house," I said.

Kate arrived later in the day, carrying a large leather

bag. She was a large woman who carried herself with an air of confidence. She always 'spoke her truth' as she liked to say. She would say what she thought and was not always politically correct, but she was never inappropriate, despite what others may have thought. She lived by the motto: *'Honesty is the best policy.'*

I greeted her at the door and was pleased to tell her we are moving to a new house. She was not surprised and told me the feeling she had at the time was very strong. I joked about the fact she was off by one day, but she simply shrugged. I quickly changed the subject and focus onto her. I asked her what she was looking for from me.

"I've been wearing contact lenses for too long and would like to do something about it. Greg seemed preoccupied and wasn't listening to what I wanted so he finally suggested it might be good for me to talk to you and learn how you have improved your eyesight." She said this with a lot of enthusiasm, and I could see she was motivated.

"Are you familiar with any vision exercises?" I asked, looking for a starting point.

"Yes, Greg gave me several exercises I have been practicing diligently for a few weeks, but they haven't helped me very much. I think there's a lot more I could be doing."

"Definitely, and it also depends on your definition of vision," I agreed. "I believe vision is far more than what you see with your eyes. It's about gaining insight into

Chapter 7 — Inner Reflections

who we are, where we are coming from and where we want to go. You already embody some of that with your ability to read people. But how much do you know about yourself. This understanding of vision goes beyond wearing glasses. But we all begin with the basics. First, we improve our physicality, so we start with eye exercises. That's where I started. I think you may have achieved this first stage and you're ready to go to the next one."

"You're right," she said and seemed pleased with what I was saying. "I want to know what my options are and what is the best path for me to take."

"The options and possibilities are limitless. When you work on expanding your consciousness you can improve your eyesight, but you're also working on your whole person – head, heart and soul. These are all connected and a change in one will enhance the others. Improving your vision will help you see the world more clearly both physically and spiritually."

"That sounds like alchemy," Kate suggested.

"What's alchemy?" I asked.

"An alchemist is someone who can turn base minerals such as lead into gold. It's a fascinating craft that became a philosophy. As you can imagine, people wanted to know more because they believed it would make them wealthy. But once they discovered it required a commitment to a lifetime of learning, few people were interested. The foundation of this knowledge was in knowing yourself before you could master the elements. Alchemy means transformation. Many who achieved their goal of changing physical matter lost interest in material things because they had learned so much about themselves.

"Are there still people who practice alchemy today?"

"I think so, but I don't know who they are or where to find them. They don't disclose themselves. The material world is no longer of significance to them."

"But we live in a physical world," I offered, very interested in what Kate had described. "It would be exciting to combine the knowing, the physical and the spiritual realms."

"Yes, for those who can achieve it, but I doubt there are many who could," Kate explained.

"Life is about balance, in the same way as staying physically resilient. We know we must stay active and exercise often in order to stay healthy, but how many people stay with it. I have met so many people who say they are on a spiritual path but never do any exercise. And then there are others, who maintain a regular exercise program and have no interest in anything spiritual."

"Exercise improves your health and well-being. One person might run marathons or work out every day in a gym. I prefer to have fun when I exercise. I enjoy riding my bike and if didn't, I would find reasons not to do it. I also like to play squash, but I'm still learning to just enjoy the game and not be so competitive. Now I'm trying to focus on the game and on doing my best. It's interesting, I feel my vision improving during a game and after a half hour I can see better than when I wore glasses. It's the same when I'm riding my bike or go for a run." I stopped and waited for Kate's response.

"Yes, I understand what you are saying," Kate said, "the same thing has happened to me after a long walk. But I did not realise my eyesight could vary, so I just assumed it was just my imagination. After listening to you, I know now it is true. The same analogy is true about our diet."

I could feel my thoughts expanding as we shared our experiences. It was as if I was expressing these ideas to myself for the first time as I explained them to Kate.

"I've read so much contradictory information about the foods we eat. Some experts say potatoes are good for you and other say, they are not. My suggestion is to let your body tell you what is good for you and what is not. Someone's health will improve on a vegetarian diet while others recognise they should eat meat at every meal. You must get in tune with your body and learn more about how foods affect your body and your mind.

"Personally, I found I had to limit the amount of red meat I ate in a week, but I don't need to give it up. I did give up coffee and alcohol. I didn't enjoy the feeling of being dazed after drinking them, so I have switched to herbal teas and hot water and feel so much better. This was my personal choice. Everyone has to decide for themselves. For some there may be adverse withdrawal symptoms. I felt it too, when I stopped drinking coffee, but the few weeks of discomfort were worthwhile. I feel so much better and I'm healthier today."

"Yes, that makes sense," agreed Kate, "and it is likely those changes helped improve your eyesight. I know it's a personal choice, but it would be difficult for me because I reach for a cup of coffee as soon as I walk in the door."

"Of course, these are habits that can be broken," I assured her. "I have some habits that are awfully hard to break. I often reach for a packet of potato chips or some chocolate when I sit down to watch television and when I finish eating them, I don't feel better. In fact, I feel worse because I see myself putting on weight. Lately, I have started to substitute carrots for chips, and I feel more satisfied. More importantly, I watch a lot less television and have become more active. I'm even taking a massage course.

"Exercising and changing our diet affect our health. Add to that the position we are in when we read. I used to read lying down in bed and found my eyes hurt by the time I was ready to go to sleep. I just put up with it because I enjoyed reading in that position. But once I made the change to sitting up, with a better reading lamp on my bedside table, I could read better and longer, and my eyes didn't tire."

Kate talked about the courses she had taken on posture and demonstrated these to me so I could improve my posture. I was very aware I slumped, especially when I was working at my computer, which involved long periods staring at the screen. I had already started taking breaks, stopping to look out the window

Chapter 7   *Inner Reflections*

to take the pressure off my eyes and decrease fatigue. Too often I forgot to correct my posture and that reminded us both to be more mindful of everything we did.

She talked about her meditation classes and the importance of being in the present and being mindful.

"In order to be fully present," she suggested, "you need to be aware of your breath. Whenever you feel stressed, stop and focus all your attention on your breath. It works every time. This is the foundation of my meditation classes." Kate then reached into her bag and took out a wooden box the size of a cigar case. She told me it was very good to be talking to someone openly and honestly. She was very impressed with my progress on my vision and my suggestions on how she could achieve similar results.

Kate then opened the box and removed a set of cards wrapped in a piece of blue silk. She placed them on the coffee table and proceeded to turn over each card one at a time. "These are my Tarot cards," she explained. "They're my tool but what I see in them really comes from my guides. Please shuffle the deck, divide them into three groups and put them on the cloth."

This was my first Tarot card reading, although I had watched while others had had them. I thought of the gypsies travelling the countryside and I was curious. The cards were larger than a regular deck of playing cards, so I had trouble shuffling them. When I set them down on the cloth, Kate instructed me to pick them up again in any order. I hesitated, hoping I picked them up correctly and gave them to her.

Kate then turned the cards over and put them into three groups of seven. "This is called a twenty-one-card spread," she explained. "The first seven cards indicate your past, the middle seven, your present and the last seven is about your future. We'll begin with your past.

"The first three cards are the King of Cups, the Tower and the World."

I looked at the illustrations on each card and noticed a person falling out of the tower.

"This card tells me; you have learned a lot of good lessons through recent crises. The other cards show you have become more confident. The Moon suggests you are being taken care of as you continue to learn and grow as a person." She talked about the Four of Pentacles, which revealed I used to be cheap or maybe overly careful with money. I told her that all she had said was true, and then she focused on the middle line of seven cards.

"The middle line is the present. The King of Pentacles and the High Priestess suggest you are moving into a new role. You will leave your current job and move into a spiritual realm. The Knight of Cups suggests you should take it slowly. The Wheel suggests you still have a lot to learn before this can happen.

"The last two cards on this line are about your intuition. The Ace of Swords indicates again you should move slowly and meditate on it." I was pleased with her reading and told her since I had had my operation, I had

Chapter 7   *Inner Reflections*

focused on meditation but lately, as I had returned to work, I had not been as diligent with my practice as I felt I should be.

"The cards are saying," Kate continued, "you must renew your faith in meditation, listen to your guides, and be grateful for the guidance both offer you.

"The top row is about your future. The middle card in this top group is the Magician, the Emperor on the left and the Four of Wands on the right. Each of these represent new opportunities for you. You will be like a Magician; picking up skills to achieve magic. The cards on either side suggest you still have much to learn and you'll have to travel far by plane before you can achieve that outcome. The Ace of Pentacles tells you that you don't have to worry about money anymore, it will all come back to you." Kate paused and asked if I had any questions.

I considered cards in the top row and said, "I've been thinking about taking a full massage course next year, but I get so tired sometimes. What do the cards suggest?"

"I see you will have the opportunity to take the massage course next year. You should look at the tiredness as just that, you get tired, but it has nothing to do with your tumour. Lots of openings will happen, just be patient."

Patience was something I still had to learn. No matter how many times I had been told to slow down, I had to see the finish line before the race was over. Meditation was helping me to slow down, but I was still anxious about the future. I was also feeling attached to my house, having lived in so many places in the past. I began to see our current home as the place where I had been born spiritually and where I was becoming more myself. Other houses had been spaces to sleep between work, but this place had become a home.

After we moved our furniture to the new house, and I saw the large open spaces and the children enjoying choosing their bedrooms with no prompting from Sara and me, my views changed and I no longer saw the old house as ours. I was very excited, when I saw the room we had chosen as a healing room, where Sara and I anticipated seeing clients and offering workshops.

Once we moved in, my weekends and evenings were taken up with tearing down old fences and replacing them further away from the house to make the backyard bigger for the children to play in. My hands were calloused from the physical work and scratched by the barbed wire. The old lawn mower we brought with us did not do well on the bigger grounds. It took me four hours to mow the lawn, so I convinced Sara we should buy a motorised lawn mower.

The previous owner had not taken care of the grounds and we wanted to plant trees. We no longer felt the land was ours to spoil. We wanted to make it an oasis for us and generations to come. We had the grounds cleaned up and after several loads of debris were removed, we built two bonfires which we all enjoyed. Sara, the children and I spent several weekends planting native gums and wattles we knew would replenish the soil so we could start a garden. We recognised it would take years before the vegetation would be established.

After a few weeks, Sara and I both decided to take a break from renovating the house and the surrounding acreage and focus on ourselves. We enrolled in an advanced Reiki course together to be held on the first weekend in November. Through this course, we found our healing energy was being fine-tuned. We told our Reiki instructor, Martha, about our new home and that we now had space for offering our own sessions to clients. She suggested we organise some open days.

"You could open your home up one day a month and it would allow people to come by and learn about Reiki and get to know you." I liked this idea but had already decided we would be offering Reiki and other modalities of healthy living. Ideally, we would have other health practitioners join us. I didn't see this as a competition and knew our guests would benefit from it. We set a date for our first open house in December.

My left eye was my weaker eye, so for a few weeks I had been using a patch over my right eye to encourage my left eye to work harder. Immediately after I began to wear a patch, I found more issues were coming to the forefront about my past. Feelings of uncertainty, loneliness and confusion were arising every time put on the patch for longer than an hour. In the beginning, I thought it might be related to moving into a new house but as the feelings intensified, I recognised it had more to do with my newfound spirituality.

One Vision

I called Ivan and described these feelings to him. I was also feeling an increased sense of responsibility. We both acknowledged these feelings were common for everyone but sadly men were not good at openly expressing them. As we explored what would attract people to a healing day, I decided I would hold a session just for men two weeks before our open house.

We had a few men sign up for the healing day, but just before the session began, both Ivan and I started to received calls from them, one by one, apologising for being unable to attend. One man had a cold, another's car did not start, and another had some urgent work he couldn't avoid, and so on. At the time we were due to start, there was just Ivan and me in the room. We had a good laugh and concluded the men in Ballarat were not ready to address their emotional and spiritual health. Greg called to remind me that Andrew Whitecross was coming back to Melbourne for another workshop and I was welcome to drive in with Kate and him. On our drive to Melbourne I told them about the dream I had the night before. I dreamed I was offering them each a bowl of curry instead of the cups of tea and biscuits they had wanted.

I found the workshop very enlightening. I was reminded I needed to be present and not worry about the past or the future. When we started to explore our dreams in a group setting, I told the group about the same dream I had recounted to Greg and Kate that morning. But as soon as I did, I realised I had not learned my lesson; I was reverting to old habits where I would jump headfirst into new situations without thinking and end up feeling hurt. I went over to speak to Andrew during the break and thanked him for allowing me to express myself to the group as well as I could. "Go easy on yourself," Andrew tutored me, "there's plenty of time for you to learn and evolve."

After the break Andrew talked more about vision and colour. In the final session we were asked to summarise what we had learned during the day. There were close to twenty people in the audience and I was going to be the last to speak. I started to think about what I would say. After the fourth person stood up to speak, Andrew stopped him and asked him how much time he had spent preparing what he was about to say. "From the moment I arrived," he confessed.

I could see I was not alone in pre-planning what I wanted to say to the group, before I had grasped what I had learned during the workshop. I really hadn't heard what the others were saying, because I had been focused on myself. I decided at that moment to actively listen and take in what each of the other participants were saying. I realised then, I was learning from each of them and they were contributing to my learning as much as Andrew did. A lot of what I wanted to say echoed the thoughts already expressed by the others, so when it came to my turn, I wasn't sure if I had anything more to add to the conversation.

"First of all," I started, "I want to tell you how impressed I am with what I have learned today, both from Andrew and from all of you. You were all open and spoke your truth. I am grateful for that and happy I decided to come today. The most important lesson I

One Vision

have learned during the past hour is to listen thoughtfully. I have also learned I should always be grateful for my talents; I do not need to be someone else. I now accept my tumour as a gift because it created the necessity for me to be open to learning about who I am and who I am meant to be."

In that moment, I had never felt so centered and happy to be alive.

It was getting dark and the streetlights were coming on as Kate and I walked to her car. Kate asked me if I was in a rush to get home.

"Not really, why?" I replied.

"I'd like to visit a Spiritualist Church that's about fifteen minutes from here. Their service starts soon and finishes at about ten o'clock. Would you like to come with me?"

"That sounds interesting," I said. "Let me call Sara to let her know I'll be home later."

I spoke to Sara, then Kate and I grabbed a snack to eat on the way to the church. We arrived at a small timber hall with an illuminated welcome sign on the front lawn. We walked through a large wooden door with carvings of the earth and sun on it. Inside, the people were dressed casually in jeans and windbreakers. I guess I had been expecting bright, colorful clothes like those worn by gypsy-type clairvoyants on television.

We assembled in a small room next to the main auditorium which was usually used for worship. Kate greeted the many people present and introduced me to them. Then, she took me to meet the minister, a woman, whom she introduced as Helen.

"Welcome," Helen said. She was an older woman in her sixties. She was smartly dressed in a long woollen dress and jacket. She had dark hair which didn't show any sign of her age; only the lines on her face gave away that the years were passing.

"I'm Joshua," I said, pausing for something more to say. "Kate told me you are in charge."

"Not quite," Helen smiled, "yes, I'm the minister of this church but I am not in charge. I'm a member of a committee that's responsible for running this church. Have you been in a Spiritualist Church before?"

"No, I haven't," I answered. "I'm Catholic but I have been to services at many Christian churches and find there are more similarities than differences."

Helen nodded. "A Catholic background makes it easier for you to understand what we do here. In this church, we communicate with spirits," she said. "We believe they are messengers from God and are here to help us along our path. They serve the planet. You also have your saints, but the difference is these spirits communicate with us."

"I do believe in spirits and have discovered my own guides during meditation sessions," I told her.

"Yes, I'm glad you're listening to them. Your spirits are here to guide you through your journey of growth,"

Helen said in a calm, peaceful manner.

I wasn't sure if I had just imagined communicating with my guides but after speaking with Helen, I was reassured and felt more certain. Kate and I sat down, and Helen spoke briefly to all those gathered there about the importance of trusting our instincts. After that, the group moved next door to where the service would take place. Chairs were placed in a circle and candles were lit in all corners of the room. There was an altar next to one of the groupings of candles but there was no special place for Helen in the circle. We were instructed to hold hands and the group said several prayers, before Helen led the group in meditation. She was guiding us into a special place when my mind went blank and I felt myself drifting above my body. I felt light and a familiar calmness came over me. I was talking with someone when I became aware that Helen was bringing us back to the room. I knew I had been in a dream-like state and the conversation left my consciousness. I opened my eyes and my mouth felt very dry. I was glad to have brought a glass of water with me from the other room. I bent down to pick it up and glanced at my watch and saw that more than an hour had passed since we first sat down.

Helen talked to us about what she witnessed during the meditation. I remembered what I learned earlier in the day and paid special attention to Helen as she spoke to each of us to see what I could learn.

When she came to me Helen said, "Joshua, do you know your guide is Native American?"

"Yes," I told her I was aware of that.

"He's offering you one of the feathers from his head dress for what you have learned up until now," said Helen, "and tells me you will have to earn the rest."

I was pleased having been acknowledged by my guide and understood I had a long way to go. I was just an apprentice in spirituality and had lots of time to learn. After the service Kate and I drove back to Ballarat.

I had a renewed sense of purpose and was heading in the right direction towards my true self. Exactly how that was going to happen would be unveiled in the next few months.

As December drew closer, I decided to complete a course in massage therapy. Before my operation I had planned to take a computer course, but no longer had any interest in studying computers, even though I was using computers on a daily basis in the office. This choice was the complete opposite.

I took some time looking for the right course for me. I hadn't heard any positive feedback on the two courses offered in Ballarat. So, being good at tackling problems I wrote to every massage school in the state of Victoria. Within a week, I had collected information on all the available courses, read through each course outline and listed their strengths and weaknesses. The course I eventually chose was the furthest away from Ballarat and the most expensive.

It was a big decision and Sara was supportive. She saw it as a new vocation for me but was getting frustrated with my inability to decide. "You have to make a decision," Sara finally said when I showed her my short-listed courses. "Trust that the right course will turn up."

"I called the woman in charge of the course and she hasn't called back."

As I uttered those words the phone rang. We looked at each other and laughed. It was the lady from the massage school. She agreed with me that massage could be combined with Reiki and Chiron healing. She described the course and by the time I hung up the phone I was convinced this was the right course for me. An added bonus was one of the course designers was the woman who had led our weekend course and whom I had found to be very caring.

Our Open House was scheduled for the following Sunday. I was looking forward to it because it gave me an opportunity to demonstrate my new-found spirituality. We had hung notices in the local health food shops and at The Silver Tree in Ballarat. Many of our new friends had already signed up.

Sara and I had transformed our lounge into a large healing space. We had set up four massage tables. People came with different therapies they wanted to share. The final count was close to fifteen people, and the four massage tables were always busy. A few people brought along their children who played happily together and gave the event a family-friendly atmosphere. The children were picking up some of the information and those who understood some of it were

Chapter 7 — Inner Reflections

explaining it to the others. In simple words, they realised the adults were doing activities to heal themselves and the planet. At the end of the day I felt good about having given our community something they wanted and needed. When everyone had left, Sara and I talked about the outcome of the day; about what had worked and what had not.

"You know," she said, somewhat hesitantly, "I think the day went well and we achieved a great deal. But I felt while we know so much, we still have more to learn for ourselves and about ourselves. So before we do this again, we need to continue to grow personally and as a couple. As we evolve spiritually, we will be able to do much more for our clients. I don't think we'll be doing these Open Houses much longer."

"Why do you say that?" I asked, pleased with Sara's thoughtfulness and optimism.

"People will grow to trust us, much sooner than I would have thought a short time ago." Her voice was filled with emotion. "Did you see how open they were when they told us what parts of their bodies hurt, and how trusting they were in our ability to help them feel better?" She was obviously pleased with the day's outcome. "But they still do not understand, we can only help repair their bodies, that true healing comes from within. They want us to do it for them, but our job is to help them understand how they can help themselves," she continued.

I agreed with her observations. It had been a good day all around. "Do you think we should set a date for the next Open House?" I asked trying to understand Sara's point of view.

"I think we can all learn more about healing from seeing people in groups like this, but are the clients getting some-benefit from it? They will become more comfortable with the services we offer. We will have to be patient and recognise this as a stepping-stone to what we want to accomplish in the future. It is up to God whether we succeed or not." I felt the same caution that Sara did and the same optimism that there was something important around the corner for us, but I couldn't see how far it would go. Would our healing sessions continue for a week, a month or a year? We would just have to wait and see.

We did not have to wait very long, changes started to happen almost immediately. Several people we had met decided to take the same massage course Sara and I had completed. I took advantage of these opportunities to talk to them about my theory regarding vision, and about the many guides that came into my life, including Edgar Cayce. A number of situations occurred that had no explanations, such as the time when the children were watching a video and it suddenly broke down. Even they understood it might have been inappropriate for them to be watching that type of program in our house.

That night, in my dream I was given a set of cards by a woman who appeared to have the respect of the community. I was told to pick two cards and to look at them. The first card was of a flower with a bright white glow emanating from its center. I interpreted it to mean I

Chapter 7 *Inner Reflections*

needed to believe in myself. It was an appropriate interpretation because I still believed others were far more spiritually gifted than I.

The second card included a written message. It said, "Sara, you are feeding him fish and chips too often." That was strange, I thought, and then I woke up with a feeling I was holding a deck of cards. I thought it might be alchemy. When I truly became aware, I realised there were not any cards in my hand.

I immediately wrote down the dream so I might talk to Sara about it later.

"I know I have to believe in myself and spirit, Sara, but I'm still questioning all these chance meetings I'm having because each one is meaningful. I think the fish and chips vision is telling me I am eating too many takeout meals. It is suggesting I become more disciplined and improve my diet. It was interesting I had a dream within a dream and actually woke up twice."

"Yes, I think those concerns have been on your mind because they are important to you," Sara assured me. "You're preparing yourself for some important changes."

"That sounds right," I said, "but I'm still amazed at how real the cards felt in my hand."

"What's the most difficult thing for you to accept about yourself?" Sara surprised me with the question.

"Probably, my ability to heal, be it myself or another person."

One Vision

"All right then," said Sara validating me, "don't deny it, just go for it!"

Christmas was approaching, and the children's attention had turned to what they wanted Santa Claus to bring them. As hard as we tried to limit the focus on materialism, it was difficult. We told them wonderful stories about the true meaning of Christmas, and we drove to Melbourne on Christmas Eve to sing Christmas carols with fifty thousand people, each with a burning candle in their hands, at the Sydney Myer Music Bowl. We talked about Jesus and his messages of living in harmony and being responsible for our own development as good people. As we talked to our children the words took on greater meaning for us too.

Universal Laws

Sara and I celebrated New Year's Eve with Ivan and Magda. They had a friend visiting from out of town. David and Melissa were happy to be spending the evening playing with their new friends too. When we arrived at their home, we took off our coats and the children immediately ran off with their playmates. Ivan ushered us into the lounge room and introduced us to their friend Peter. He was relaxing with a hot drink in his hands.

I shook his hand and felt at ease with his strong, friendly grip. He was a tall, lanky man with dark hair and a boyish face. Magda went to prepare some herbal tea for us, while Ivan explained how he and Peter had met.

"Peter is a member of the Association for Research and Enlightenment, A.R.E., in Melbourne and has been studying Edgar Cayce's work for more than ten years as well as numerology." I was very impressed with this young man's credentials.

"I have been reading a lot of Edgar Cayce myself," I told Peter. "But I don't know anything about numerology. I'm very interested in learning more about it," I said, feeling very comfortable speaking to him.

"We know numbers affect our lives and numerology is the study and practice of it. I would be happy to demonstrate it to you later this evening," Peter said enthusiastically.

We enjoyed our dinner. The meal Magda had prepared for us showed she was a wonderful cook. The conversation centred on the highlights of the year for each of us and we lamented over how quickly time flies.

"So much has changed for Sara and me this year. I wonder now, especially at the end of a year, where this personal development is leading. I wish I had a view of the path that lies ahead and some reassurance I'm on the right one," I said, almost to myself.

"Maybe I can help you, Joshua. Let me show you how numerology works," enthused Peter. "What month and day were you born?"

"The third of February," I replied.

"What year were you born?"

"Nineteen sixty-one."

Peter did some quick calculations in his head before

he spoke, "If you add the numbers in the month, day and year, you get twenty-two. The two numbers in twenty-two when added together make four. That is a good starting point. The number four suggests you're a very practical person and before you do anything you must know how it works and the results you're going to have."

"That sounds exactly like him," Sara agreed.

"It also means," Peter continued, "you're very serious and risk-averse. You don't like taking chances; you work hard, are focused and tenacious"

"That was true a few years ago," I told Peter, "but I've changed. I shifted my priorities and what you see in my numbers may not apply now."

"I appreciate that, and you find out more the further you go into the numbers. Your birth year changes the outcome," explained Peter. "Let me give you an example. We're heading into the year, 1995. The numbers of this year add up to twenty-four, which pares down to six. Six signifies the family, so I suggest throughout the world people will be more attentive to relationships and will be spending more time at home in the coming year."

"For you personally, we'll combine the day and month of your birth and the numbers will determine what will be in store for you next year. Three for your birthday, add two for the month of you birth and six for the new year. That adds up to eleven. In numerology, eleven, twenty-two and thirty-three are called master numbers. They carry special significance and are often not even reduced further to a base number. In your case, next year would be what we refer to as being an eleven or two year for you.

"An eleven or two year means, next year, you will be emerging from your protected life and becoming more accepting of what you are capable of doing. Given this is happening in a six-year, as I explained before, I would see 1995, will be a year of service to your family as well as others, for you Joshua."

"That's remarkable," I said, "I will be taking a massage course next year and once I have completed the course, I plan on making my services more widely available. I will be offering therapies like Reiki, along with other healing modalities which will have more credibility and better results.

Peter was listening intently and said, "I think you will become less skeptical and more appreciative of wonders you cannot see or verify."

I agreed with Peter. I was always looking for logical explanations for everything I was learning and yet I felt more confident about my new career. I likened myself to scientists who continue to have faith knowing some things cannot be proven in a controlled environment but were nonetheless true. There was room for different belief systems to co-exist and learn from each other. I believed, you are able to question your faith while recognising the miracle of the universe and the universe of miracles.

Chapter 8 — Universal Laws

Peter explained we each have four pinnacles and four challenges in our lifetime. A pinnacle is your achievement of a level of understanding and a challenge is the difficulty you must face. The first in each of the categories was birth, when you first become aware. This is calculated by deducting your birth date from thirty-six. I realised for me this number was thirty-two, the age at which my tumour was discovered. For me, that was the year of my awakening. The next three pinnacles and challenges occur exactly nine years apart, which meant my final pinnacle and challenge would occur when I was fifty-nine.

Peter explained this using my numerological story. "Joshua is currently experiencing his second pinnacle, which combines the three for his day of birth and the eight for the year of his birth, which gives the result eleven-two. This represents a partnership, which could be at home or in business. Joshua, your numbers reveal you will be embarking on a partnership and your challenge is to learn to share, co-operate and develop patience. An eleven-two pinnacle also indicates a need for spirituality. This may appear to be a hurdle for you, but these major changes will build deeper understandings, both within you and with others. From what you have told me about yourself, I can see this corresponds with everything that's going on in your life right now. You will continue to face greater challenges, and what they are, will depend on how we use the numbers. For example, instead of adding the numbers, we could subtract them. When we subtract three from eight, we get five. Five becomes your second challenge. Five indicates a deep craving for personal freedom. If you don't feel free you become resentful and irritated. It's important you believe you are free to do what you want and are not being restricted by either family or by the career opportunities available to you."

"I understand what you're telling me and that is how I've been feeling," I confirmed, grateful for Peter's explanation. "At times I believe both my family and my job are putting limitations on my spiritual journey. I have an urge to pack up and go on this other path I am meant to follow. But at the same time, I recognise my family are the most important people in my life and my work allows me to provide for them."

Ivan interrupted because he felt a need to clarify for me some of what Peter had said. "Peter is saying you should be aware you are heading on the right path. Opportunities will arise but you need to be ready and recognise them when they do. Just be patient. Right now, you are preparing yourself for what is inevitable."

I was so excited by what I was hearing. "What you're saying is it all comes down to my being patient. I just have to be patient until I achieve that level of patience."

We all laughed at what I had just uttered.

"I think," Ivan continued, "it comes down to becoming aware of the reason we chose to be born at this specific time. Where we are today is the cumulation of the many decisions we made in this and previous lifetimes. It's the Law of Cause and Effect."

"The law of what?" Sara asked Ivan before I did.

Chapter 8 — Universal Laws

"Cayce referred to it as the Universal Laws. These are the laws or principles that bind the universe together. They're a collection of naturally enforced rules that guide everything we do. The first of these is the Principle of Cause and Effect, which states we get back what we put out. If we do something wrong today or in a previous lifetime, there will be consequences. For example, if we steal in the present, we may find in the next life people are taking things from us."

"I've heard about that before," I said. "It's called karma. But it doesn't mean we are all doomed by our past lives. For instance, we may have killed someone in a previous life and didn't get caught. Does that mean we'll get punished for the crime in the next life?"

"That would depend on why we killed. Was it to protect our family or to profit from the killing? Besides, karma isn't necessarily fatalistic. We can choose how we respond to every situation that arises," Peter explained.

"Cayce's vision showed before we are born, we choose our parents because we have lessons to learn from them based on our past life experiences and circumstances. Numerology and astrology can provide some of the clues to help us understand what lessons we need to learn. They can help us learn what our life's purpose is and decide how we can achieve it in our daily lives. It helps us choose our careers and what we want to focus our lives work on," continued Ivan.

I was considering what they were saying and trying to apply it to my own life. My job allowed me to talk with a variety of people about their finances. My personal integrity had a direct influence on how truthful they were. I received back what I put into action. I was more successful because of my honesty.

But what about my past lives? I considered why I had chosen my parents and the country of my birth. "If we choose our parents because of past life circumstances, how does that play out in terms of hereditary aspects and environmental factors, for instance my skin color or where I live? Surely, they effect who I am today."

"I don't see these as conflicting views," Peter suggested. "Why would we not choose our parents for all the reasons we need to learn from them? The same would be true for everything else; where we live and the opportunities available to us."

These ideas were new to me and yet they felt surprisingly familiar and comfortable. "I can see how the Law of Cause and Effect could be applied," I mused.

"This is just one of the laws Cayce identified, and you've heard about all of them at one time or another," Ivan explained. "Another one is like attracts like, suggesting you will meet the right people at the right time to move you towards your destination. As you can see you are attracting the best people into your life, right now. They are helping you evolve and move forward on your path. Most people will call this chance, luck or coincidence. However, they are wrong. According to the Universal Laws, nothing happens by chance. Everything happens for a reason. Every person you are meeting has appeared so you can learn from them and they, from you."

I considered what Ivan was saying and had to ask, "Is there some enormous plan at work here, to create all these occurrences for just one person, let alone the billions of people around the world? How else would this be possible?"

"Not at all," Ivan persisted. "We say God has infinite wisdom. We do not have to know how it works, but based on the miracles we see each day, we must have faith and accept the infinite is at work. The more we examine the coincidences in our day-to-day lives, the more we become aware of how frequently they occur."

Sara was also intrigued by everything she was hearing and asked, "There are so many people in the world and through so many generations, how would past lives be kept in order?"

"Let me try to answer your question," Magda joined the conversation. "My understanding of past lives is, previously, we chose our next lives very carefully between each reincarnation. But throughout the centuries we seem to be reincarnating faster and faster so the time between each lifetime becomes shorter. According to Cayce, most souls have had tens if not hundreds of reincarnations.

"This has become confusing for some because they've had less time to adjust and incorporate past learnings from lifetime to lifetime. This might also be why so many people are unclear about their life's purpose. They are still trying to deal with lessons from

One Vision

past lifetimes as well as the lessons of this life. This can lead to harmony or chaos, depending on your ability to cope with uncertainty."

The children came in from the yard and we took a break from this intense conversation. "Can we watch a video please?" one of them called out, seeing there may not be much resistance from us, as we might want to continue talking. They made themselves comfortable on the couch in the study as another put on a Disney video. Magda suggested we meditate while the children were busy watching the video. We agreed, feeling very comfortable with each other. Ivan led us through some Cayce recommended pre-meditation exercises. We sat in a circle and went through various forms of breathing techniques as the room became quiet and peaceful.

The perfume of essential oils floated through the room although I did not see any signs of them burning as the room became dark. I closed my eyes and my thoughts went to all the tasks I had to do around the house next week. I realised Sara would be equally busy taking care of the children and helping her parents. Then I relaxed and focused only on my breath and felt my mind become quiet and my attention focused on the inside of my eyelids as if a projector had been turned on.

I heard someone communing with me. They were telling me I did not have to make all the choices in my life by myself. I had had guidance in the past and would continue to have it. I felt a heavy weight fall from my shoulders. I had been wondering if a spiritual path was suitable for me. I saw the word 'TRUST' appear on the screen. It made me feel secure knowing that my guides would be taking care of me. I felt my body vibrate and I was aware we weren't alone, but I wasn't afraid, instead I felt comforted.

We completed the meditation and opened our eyes all at once and at that precise moment, the clock on the wall struck twelve. We wished each other a very happy New Year. The children had managed to stay awake until midnight but were tired and were happy to go to bed even before the movie ended.

When the children had settled down, we talked about what occurred during our meditation. I described to the group that I had recognised I must have more trust in my choices.

"Most people don't really understand how they make important choices," Magda interjected. "For some people it is all about what work they do and how much money they make. I don't think these are important choices. The real choice is whether we choose a God-centered, spiritual path, or an ego-centered, material path.

"That doesn't mean money isn't necessary. We should expect a fair exchange for our talents and services, but it's the intent of our actions, to serve rather than just to make money, that will determine the path we follow."

"What I have found," I said directly to Magda, "is when my intentions were pure money appeared, to allow me to do what I wanted."

"The Universe let you know your choices were

spiritually based because you followed your heart rather than your mind. If you are in tune with the Universe, your needs will be met, no more and no less than you need.

"Many businesses believe money is the true sign of success. Their marketing story may demonstrate they care about the community, but beneath their façade they are in an ego-based competition with their rivals."

I was very much aware as an accountant, my objectives were usually to make as much money as possible for my firm. But recently, I had felt a change in my attitude and behavior. I had become more interested in helping my clients achieve their goals and was surprised these actions had also helped the firms profit line. When my intent changed, everyone, including myself benefited.

We spent the night at Ivan and Magda's home. When we sat down for breakfast the next morning, we continued our conversation from the night before. It was a new year, and a new beginning. This morning, we found ourselves deep in a discussion about past lives. I had so many questions, I did not know where to begin.

"Peter, you say we've all had many past lives. How many and when did it all start?" I asked the group.

Peter swallowed his food, wiped his mouth and said, "According to Cayce, people arrived on Earth some twenty-five to thirty thousand years ago. There were five groupings of people, each with a different skin colour, including white, brown, black, yellow and red.

Chapter 8 — Universal Laws

Most people are familiar with the story of Atlantis. Atlantis was a very sophisticated society powered by the energy derived from crystals.

"The souls that inhabited Earth came to experience living in a physical environment, and over the years they lost their ability to return to the spirit worlds from which they came. They - developed a fascination for physical pleasures and lost their spirituality. They became greedy and the spirits have returned to Earth time and again to remedy this change.

"Atlantis became a technologically advanced society, like ours is today. The advancements occurred faster than the Atlanteans could understand them. It is thought Atlantis was destroyed by massive explosions when the crystals powering their civilisation became over-worked. Most of us have been reincarnating since the Atlanteans made their first mistakes. We have been trying to rectify those errors and learn the lessons we were meant to learn ever since.

"As to the number of reincarnations we may have had, that will vary for everyone. But if you consider the length of time since Atlantis, on average it would be hundreds of lifetimes and each one has taught our spirit something, accruing to where we are today."

"Are we at the end of our past lives?" Sara asked, more and more intrigued by what she heard, as was I.

"It is possible for us to learn all the lessons we need and not have any debts owing from previous lives. When that happens, we will be given the choice to come back to Earth and help others complete their journey, by learning all they must or to move on to some other place or dimension.

"What's interesting is we tend to find the exact person to teach us the lessons we need to learn. For instance, if you were interested in Cayce's work in a previous life, you will search out the people who have the same pursuit in this life. Some of these people will be individuals who had readings from Cayce in person or who studied his work," Ivan said.

"Think about the people who matter to you most. How did you meet them? Why did you feel a connection with them?" Peter asked.

"That's how I felt when I first met Ivan," I said. "I felt as though I already knew him, and we were picking up our friendship from where we left off at some other time."

Peter looked intensely at both of us before speaking, "I don't doubt you have spent several lifetimes together. I know Ivan and now I'm getting to know you and Sara, I would say sometimes Ivan would have been enforcing laws and you would have been breaking them, especially if you didn't agree with him."

"That sums it up well," Magda agreed.

"You are both working together now because they both have lessons to learn," Peter continued. "Ivan, you need to learn to let go, and Joshua will show you how to do that. Joshua, you have to learn to stay within the boundaries and stop climbing fences. Ivan can teach you how you work within the law."

"I can do that, as long as the law makes sense to me," I quipped, knowing Peter had struck a chord.

Peter put a few of his books in a bag for me to borrow and read. After I had finished with them, I would return them to Ivan. I thanked him and told him I would start reading during the holidays. Sara and the children were going to spend a week with her parents while I stayed at home to look after the animals and finish some work around the house. I was looking forward to some time alone.

On the way home, Sara and I talked about how much we enjoyed our evening with Ivan and Magda. "It was certainly interesting. It's going to take time for me to digest all I learned, and yet so much of what was discussed seemed familiar to me."

"I feel the same way. I wonder how our lives crossed in the past?" Sara wondered aloud as we drove the rest of the way home in silence, contemplating the possibilities.

Sara and the children were leaving in the morning to stay with her parents for a week, so after the children went to bed, we prepared ourselves to meditate. Before we started, Sara took out the bag Magda had given her for Christmas. "Magda gave me some Rune stones," she said removing a flat stone with an arrow etched into it from the bag. "Magda said these stones can help you overcome your fears and focus you on your path." There was a book of explanations in the bag too. She looked up the stone, and added, "The arrow represents the rune of the courage warrior. With everything that's ahead of us, this year, we'll need this."

When I reached into the bag, I could feel at least twenty stones. I took one out and put it on the table. It was inscribed with the letter 'H'. Sara looked up the stone in her book and read the description to me, "This rune stone represents disruption. The next few days will be a little chaotic and things might not go as planned. However, whatever happens will help your spiritual growth."

"Perhaps something will happen while you're away," I remarked, not really trusting what Sara had read.

Sara took the explanation more seriously. "Just be sure to stay safe and protected while we're away. Make sure you say the prayers of protection, both for you and the house. We're both learning so much, so fast, we must be careful to clear any negative energy surrounding us."

I was amazed at how comfortable Sara had become about spiritual matters and her understanding of the need to protect ourselves from opposing forces. Her belief system was evolving and, while I was still skeptical, she was accepting. During our meditation, I felt the need for protection again. I imagined a large golden spiral growing out of the top of my head and extending into sky. I was now used to my body vibrating and knew it was letting me know I was protected and being guided. I drifted off into a deep sleep knowing I was on a journey.

Chapter 8 — *Universal Laws*

Sara and the children had a long drive ahead of them, so they left early the next morning. After waving them good-bye, I went back to bed and picked up one of the books Peter had loaned me. I was so engrossed in the book I did not notice the time. It was mid-morning before I had showered and dressed ready to take the dog for a walk.

I walked the four hundred metres to the end of our driveway which opened out onto the highway. It had rained during the night but now the sky was clear, and the sun was shining. It was a pleasant walk and, on the way back home, I let the dog off the leash. I enjoyed watching her savour her freedom, running in every direction but always back to me. As we neared the house, she slowed down and walked deliberately in front of me.

I was reaching to open the sliding glass door when a slight tapping sound distracted me. I was shocked to see a large brown snake tapping on the door with its head, near my feet. I froze. My first thought was to get the dog away from the house. She was only a year old, but she had not seemed to notice the snake, so I grabbed her by the collar and put her in the yard. Then, I headed to the front door. By the time I had walked through the house to the back door, the snake was gone. A wave of fear swept over me. I was afraid to go outside and I felt like a prisoner in my own home. I tried to ignore the fear so I went to the kitchen to make an early lunch which I hoped would settle my nerves. When I walked into the kitchen, I found a pool of water on the floor that appeared to be coming from an old freezer in the corner.

I remembered the rune stone and realised these were the disruptions it had foretold. I cleaned up the floor and called a neighbourhood store to order a new freezer. I had never bought a major appliance before without comparison shopping, but now, feeling captive inside my house I was tired of the turmoil, so I did.

I sat quietly and meditated before I was ready to venture outside. I lit a candle and closed my eyes. My attention was focused on the snake. I slowed down my breathing, but my mind returned to the earlier incidents.

Suddenly, it occurred to me I had not set up the safeguards for the house Sara had reminded me to do. I had been letting Sara ask God to keep us and our home safe. I was aware of a snake spirit that flows through all snakes and connects them to the Universe. I invited this spirit to make my house and yard free of snakes, allowing them to use the area at the end of the paddock. This request would give them their own space and I would have mine. Then I asked for protection for the house and everything in it while Sara was away.

I learned a lesson and I was grateful. I walked outside to check on the dog and to make sure the snake was gone. I strode around feeling quite safe. As I was making my way back to the house, a delivery van arrived with the freezer I had ordered earlier. While the delivery man was setting up the freezer and removing the old one, I told him about my experience with the snake. "Should have killed it straight way. They always come back," he said. But I did not agree. I knew the snake had come to teach me a lesson and it would not return. Over the course of the next few days, I put up some more fences, cleaned up the garden, and mowed the lawn to a height where a snake could be seen, just in case.

I read Peter's books on spirituality every evening and thought a great deal about the coincidences in my life. I read when you make eye contact with someone, you should be open to the possibility that further connections with them may have; these acquaintances may have a message for you or help you to learn a life's lesson.

Each day I noticed changes in how I felt and thought. I called Ivan to share my progression with him. "This week I have learned I am continually releasing fears," I explained. "Incidents have occurred during my time alone; firstly, the snake appeared, then the freezer broke down and I have been hearing noises around the house."

Ivan suggested these worries may be linked to Sara driving alone to Albury, with the children. Then he said, "Edgar Cayce said love casts out all fear. Once we are rid of all our fears, only love is left. Our goal is to have only love."

"During this week I have been given lessons for my spiritual growth," I said, "I'm starting to have more faith in myself and a stronger belief in the spirit world. I'm less dependent on others and more self-assured."

"The final step is to share your new-found beliefs with the world," Ivan added instinctively. "When you're feeling dependent on others you feel vulnerable and you want people to take care of you. Once you are self-sufficient, you are taking responsibility for your own life. Well done. In the next stage, you will come to the realisation you are here to help others find their own true selves, using that spark of divinity in all of us; where everything is possible, and things happen."

"What do you mean things happen?" I asked.

"I believe we can overcome the need to die and be born again in order to learn our life's lessons. Jesus showed us we can overcome death. By raising our level of consciousness, we can complete the lessons we came here to learn," Ivan said confidently.

"I can't say I'm not afraid of snakes now," I said honestly. "And I'm sure I still have a lot of lessons to learn."

"Certainly, but you have made a start," Ivan replied. "The more people who begin a spiritual journey, the sooner we will get to the hundredth monkey, when this collective consciousness will help to release old fears."

It had been a worthwhile conversation with Ivan. When Sara arrived home the following week, I described what happened to me while she was away and what I learned. She was surprised and told me she had a similar experience. She had known she had to be less dependent on her parents and during her stay, she finally felt on equal footing with them. The end result had been a new respect on both sides.

We had both progressed in learning the lessons we needed, even when we were apart. This reaffirmed for me once again that Sara and I were meant to be together, despite each of us being on our own a personal path. We were always reevaluating our relationship and were pleased it was continuously evolving. It was exactly at times like these when our personal journeys would zig zag away from each other but eventually move together stronger than ever.

"I'm still unclear about how Jesus and reincarnation go together?" I asked Sara one night, reflecting on my Christian upbringing.

"I read a little about this while I was away," Sara said, "the author suggested Jesus had to go through the same process of living through several reincarnations before he chose to be born in Bethlehem. In some of his past reincarnations he was one of the people responsible for writing some of the Old Testament passages and was the first to achieve divinity. That is referred to as Christ Consciousness. According to Jesus, everyone can achieve the same and more."

"That's confusing," I said. "On the one hand, we should believe in our own divinity. But then the Church instructs us to follow Jesus, the Messiah; to believe we can accomplish what Jesus did goes beyond just believing in yourself."

"It goes back to intent," Sara offered, enjoying our exchange, and trying hard to find a solution for both of us. "Thinking you are better than someone else is about your ego. But to be Christ-like means to have humility and a desire to help others help themselves. That's very difficult and we have a lifetime to work it out."

One Vision

For the second week of our new year holiday, Sara and I took the children camping. It was good to leave our everyday lives behind and enjoy each other's company. David and Melissa had missed me although they had enjoyed the attention and love their grandparents had showered on them. Their visit to Albury was the longest time we had spent away from each other since my operation and I was amazed at how wonderfully they were growing.

Before I went back to work, after the Christmas break, I went to Melbourne for another MRI to be sure the tumour had not grown. I had hoped the work I had done on my personal growth would also help reduce the tumour. When the doctor told me there had been no change, I was very disappointed, instead of being happy because I did not have to be hospitalised. Bit by bit, I began to recognise the gift I was handed and decided to follow the doctor's advice to be tested again in six months.

I was not looking forward to going back to work and had a distinct feeling I would not be working for my firm for much longer. I was now leading more vision workshops and I felt good about the direction my new career was going. I had even purchased a colour machine, similar to Greg's, that I wanted to use on myself and on others.

The Sunday before I was due to return to work, Sara and I held another successful Open House. We felt drained by the end of the day, but still decided to have one more Open House before we decided about our next steps. We knew the Open House concept would lose its appeal quickly, but it was by opening our home we both learned the best ways to deliver our services, individually or in collaboration.

That night, I dreamed the Pope had died of a heart attack in New Zealand. I had mixed emotions. In my dream I felt sad he had died but understood his death was a necessary change. Sara and I wanted to go to the funeral, but I realised I first had to change my clothes. I actually woke up in the middle of the dream, in the middle of the night, and thought about the dream. I decided the Pope represented my old beliefs and having to change my clothes meant I was still releasing my fears around what other people were thinking about the changes in me.

I went back to sleep, and immediately dreamed I was driving down the road and the car went off a bridge. During the fall, I thought, "Oh no, not again!" When I woke up the next morning, I could see the same image in my head, but this time I missed the bridge and was driving down a sunny road. It was time for me to move on.

One Vision

A Matter of Timing

I started my massage course at the University of Ballarat in early February. I had been working hard at the accounting practice for several weeks now, so this course was a pleasant change and I was looking forward to the new challenges it would provide. As I drove onto the campus, I thought about the years I had spent at the university working on my business degree. I passed by the small dam where I would swim between lectures on hot days. I noticed there were some newer buildings and the university appeared more formal than it had when I was last there.

I studied the map and found my way to the classroom. I chose a seat near the front of the class, as the facilitator, Kerrie introduced herself and explained her background in sports massage. She wore a blue tracksuit with some interesting logos embroidered on the jacket. She looked as if she did a lot of weight training.

There were sixteen students in the class, but only three other men. We took turns going around the group introducing ourselves. One man, who looked to be in his sixties said he wanted to learn massage to work on his horses. Another fellow, who was about my age, had a beard and wore glasses, looked familiar to me and I had the distinct feeling I had met him before.

When it came to the third man's turn to introduce himself, he stood up, and with a great deal of confidence, addressed the group. "Hi everyone, my name is Brian. I'm here because I'm interested in learning massage therapy to help others." He had a short, grey beard and a sparse amount of hair on his head. "I enjoy learning new things," he continued, "and I think this course will help me understand myself as well as how I can be of service to the community. I'd like to get to know you all and I hope we'll have fun too. This is quite a change for me as I'm a technological guy and have worked with computers throughout my career."

When it was my turn, I described how I planned to combine massage therapy with several other healing modalities I was also learning. I told my classmates I did not have any knowledge of anatomy, so I was aware I was facing a steep learning curve, but I was looking forward to it. Kerrie thanked us and said she was looking forward to teaching us. She explained there would be five examinations, three of which were pen and paper tests on anatomy and physiology, and the other two would be practical exams. We were asked to

Chapter 9 — A Matter of Timing

keep a logbook of all the massages we did both in class and on other people. She gave us a heavy textbook we were required to study in detail. We acknowledged this was a serious course.

"Massage," Kerri began her lecture, "is extremely beneficial for a person's overall care. It relieves tension, increases joint movement, improves blood and lymphatic circulation, aids the digestive system and helps balance the nervous system." She continued to explain the function of each organ in our body.

The first lecture went well, and my mind was filled with new, exciting information. It felt like learning a new language. I told Sara about the class and the man in the group that reminded me of someone, but I did not know who. Three weeks later, on the morning of the second weekend class, I discovered who it was.

After our introductions, the man with the beard, Ed, remarked he thought the previous class had been as easy as roller blading. His attempt at humour fell flat since his classmates had already put in hours of study. It was then I noticed his mannerisms, and even his appearance reminded me of myself a few years ago. I no longer had a beard or wore glasses, but this perception made me feel uncomfortable.

He was also interested in getting to know me and wanted to work on projects together. I mentioned this to Kerrie during our break.

"Look at it as a positive sign," Kerrie assured me. "Obviously, you have changed your appearance but perhaps this encounter is showing you there's also been a change in your attitude. You seem to have come a long way. When you see yourself in Ed, you should be pleased you're no longer that person." I agreed with her. I did not avoid him after that and by lunch time he no longer annoyed me.

After lunch, we went back into the classroom to find eight massage tables set up for the practical part of the program. However, someone had stacked them on top of each other, four to a group. We laughed and wondered who among us was the practical joker. We had our suspicions, but it didn't really matter because it had set the tone for our bonding.

Kerrie described the keystrokes that applied to the massage. "The basic stroke is effleurage. It consists of long gliding strokes covering the entire area to be massaged. Its purpose is to warm the muscles and stimulate venous and lymphatic circulation. The other primary stroke is petrissage, or kneading. It consists of the rhythmic lifting and squeezing of the fleshy parts of the body. This movement pumps nutrients through muscle tissue and eliminates waste such as lactic acid." We spent the afternoon learning several techniques and getting to know each other.

I was very busy, working four days a week at my office and studying in the evenings. I was also looking forward to our next Open House, the following Sunday so I could practice using energy to heal. When people heard the sessions offered on the day were free, seven new people showed up. Each seemed to know at least one other person there and this created an atmosphere of

Chapter 9 *A Matter of Timing*

camaraderie.

Overall, the day did not go as well as the previous Open House. Very few people came prepared to assist with any therapies, so Sara and I were kept busy doing it all, for the entire day. When everyone left, we both had headaches and used white light to clear the house of negative energy. We decided this had been our last Open House.

That night I dreamed Sara and I had sold a two-story house and bought an old run-down one. I was suspicious because we had paid too much, and my clothes were still sitting in boxes in one of the bedrooms. I took a bus to my original house, to try to get it back.

The next morning, I phoned Ivan to talk with him about the dream and the previous days' events.

"It seems to me," said Ivan, "your dream is reinforcing what you already know. The old house represents what happened yesterday, the old way of doing things. Your higher consciousness, represented by the original two-story house, is telling you that you need to use your skills more effectively. The fact you took a bus is interesting because it denotes group consciousness. I think the dream is telling you to review your reasons for organising the Open House events and suggests their purpose is over."

"I envisioned holding an Open House would let people experience the various modalities of therapies we have to offer and demonstrate how these treatments could help them feel better," I explained.

"What do you see, right now, as your ideal life?" Ivan asked, inviting me to be more focused.

"Right now," I said, "I would like to help people learn to help themselves. I would like to leave my accounting practice and work full time teaching people about alternative ways to achieve healthy lifestyles."

"Why don't you just do it?" suggested Ivan.

"Like you!" I exclaimed, "I can't afford to leave my job right now. Perhaps in a few years."

"I see your point. We're both in work we don't enjoy anymore. Our hearts aren't in it. We go to work to earn money because we have family responsibilities." With that, Ivan changed the subject, "I was going to call you just before you called me. There is a talk being given this Thursday evening at 'The Silver Tree' bookstore and I wondered if you would like to go with me. The speaker is coming from Melbourne and will be teaching about channeling and the need for protection during channeling sessions. It might be timely given what happened yesterday."

I agreed to meet him at the bookstore just before eight o'clock on Thursday.

It was a warm, clear night with a full moon when I arrived, and I was pleased to see Ivan again. "The others are already upstairs," Ivan said. "The talk will begin in a few minutes."

I was surprised to discover the speaker was Helen, whose seminar I had taken a few months ago. She

Chapter 9   *A Matter of Timing*

recognised me and smiled. There was a candle, incense and flowers around the room. "Welcome everyone," Helen began. "It's good to see so many of you here tonight. I am here to talk about channeling, which has become a very popular topic to discuss lately. As you know, the earth is going through some tremendous transformations. More and more people believe they are surrounded by guides and spirits and would like to communicate with them.

"Not all guides and spirits contribute to our higher good, so we must be careful when

choosing with whom we associate and why we want to communicate with them in the first instance. Do any of you communicate with guides?" More than half of the thirty or so people in the gathering raised their hands, including me.

"So, I ask you," Helen continued, "Why are you communicating with your guides? Is it to gain greater insights about yourself and the world? Is it to help you feel good about yourself, or to justify something you're doing? I implore you to make sure any communication with a spirit must be, and I repeat, must be, for the highest purpose and not to satisfy a personal whim.

"Before you begin any type of communication with your guides, you need to be one hundred per cent certain you're safe. You can prepare your environment and tune yourself in to be open to your guides with prayer, or by using flowers, candles, or oils. I always begin by asking Mother-Father-God to place me in a bubble of white light under the protection of Jesus. Tonight, I ask protecting angels to surround this building for our safety and angels to escort undesirable energies to a place of higher evolution. Now, I ask my personal guides and angels to provide me with the highest good.

"When you begin to channel you must stay in control at all times. For many, channeling is a way to get in touch with their higher self, so the insights that occur during a channeling session are a combination of messages from your guides and your higher thoughts. When channeling, you are tapping into universal consciousness which is the part of you that is connected to everyone else."

I noted Helen was placing far less emphasis on channeling of spirits and more importance on getting in contact with your true self. I had a sense she was suggesting you could channel your true self to receive guidance for a more meaningful life. The best way to get in touch with yourself was through meditation, because when your conscious mind is quieted, you can hear your higher self.

Helen was concerned too many people were attempting to channel spirits without the skills to create protective boundaries. "Be careful about the messages you're getting because you can't be certain of the source of that information." She spoke with tremendous honesty for almost an hour and then took questions.

"Do you ask for protection for all members of your household when you communicate with your guides?" came a question from the second row.

Chapter 9 — A Matter of Timing

"I do not ask for protection just for people, but also for the animals in my surroundings," replied Helen. "I can recall one time, a family was meditating, and their dog snapped its leg in a freak accident in the middle of the meditation. The family realised afterwards they had not included the animal in their request for protection and were therefore responsible for the dog's welfare. They decided to have the dog's leg fixed, despite the expense.

"I ask for protection and healing for myself, then for my immediate family by name, next I ask for anyone in my immediate surroundings and after that for everyone I know who needs it. Does anyone else have another question?" she asked.

Ivan raised his hand, "You talk about guides and angels. Is there a difference between them?"

"That's an excellent question." Helen replied. "Let me start by saying I believe they're different. Our guides have lived on Earth before. They may even be a soul mate or a loved one who was here in physical form and is now a spirit who has stayed with you to guide you on your path.

"Angels, on the other hand, are not of an earthly form, although there have been exceptions. Sometimes, angels have been known to take physical form. Angels often help with a specific task, or they may protect or escort. They can also heal, provide insights or help you learn. You can ask angels to help you find love or peace."

Helen concluded her address with a short meditation designed to contact each of our guardian angels.

For the next few months, I was busy with work at the accountancy firm and the massage course which I attended every third weekend. The prankster, from the first weekend continued to play practical jokes. On one weekend, we were about to apply powder for foot Reflexology, when one of the students spilled powder all over herself because there was a hole at the bottom of the can. Another time, a student laid down on the massage bed and found the pillow covered in flour. Since I hadn't experienced any 'accident' I became one of the suspects for causing them.

My meditations had become an important focus of my days. I was getting good results; feeling more balanced and centered, I was also getting clearer insights into myself and my life. I was trusting myself and what the future held. I felt I would be leaving my job in about two years but would also question the financial wisdom of doing so. The insights I received were that I would be looked after. I knew I would not be wealthy, but I would never go hungry. Sara and I realised we had to manage our expenses by using our credit cards less and living within our means.

I received a call from a woman in Bendigo. She introduced herself as Shirley and said she had heard at the Adult Education Centre in Ballarat that I was offering eye courses and asked if I could organise one in Bendigo. I was excited at the thought of leading one of my courses outside Ballarat and agreed to do it if she could sign up six participants for the weekend. We

Chapter 9 — A Matter of Timing

chose a date in August and I agreed to send her the necessary literature and pricing.

When I put the phone down, I had the distinct feeling I had turned another corner. I was feeling optimistic and while I was out shopping I bought a raffle ticket. It was for a worthy cause and the first prize was a beautiful blue car. A numerologist had predicted a new blue car was in my future and I felt this raffle was an omen.

The raffle was to be drawn on Saturday and I was positive I would win. I was so convinced I had even decided to immediately sell our small car after we took ownership of the new one. My belief was reinforced by my meditations. Even Sara believed we had the winning ticket. On Saturday we were disappointed because we didn't win. The lesson for me was I should not use my meditations for financial gain.

I was studying hard preparing to undertake the first of the three anatomy examinations. Both Brian and I had an academic background, and as most of the questions had multiple choice answers, we both completed the two-hour paper in under an hour. We had scheduled a squash game after the test and made an early start.

"What else do you do in your spare time?" I asked him on the way to the court.

"I teach a Tai Chi class at the local Adult Education Centre," Brian said in an unassuming manner.

"Really!" I exclaimed. "I've also given some courses there."

"What types of courses?" asked Brian.

"My course is for reducing the need for eyeglasses. I have offered it three times and rather than being paid, I have been given credit. I've been considering taking the Tai Chi course but didn't know you were the instructor."

"Now you know, does that mean you won't be taking it?" he said jokingly.

We were walking onto our court, and I held the door open for Brian. Following behind him, I became serious. "In fact, I feel Tai Chi would be a suitable complement to massage and would help me become more centred."

"It would certainly do that," Brian said, as he began his stretching exercises. "It is a fitting match. My course is an introduction to Tai Chi."

I signed up for his course, the next time I was at the Adult Education Centre and learned how the movements completed certain patterns. It was difficult for me to balance my body and I could not follow the flow of the steps. It took a lot of concentration. Brian and I became friends and began exchanging massages and studied anatomy together. As we spent more time together, I found Brian had a great sense of humour and discovered he was our practical joker.

Brian was also interested in other therapies, especially in the effect of light therapy.

"Why don't you come around to my house on Wednesday evening and I'll give you a demonstration?" I suggested. On Wednesday night, Brian, his wife

Chapter 9 *A Matter of Timing*

Cathy, whom Sara had previously met at several events, and three of their friends came to our home for that purpose.

I had set up five chairs in a row about two metres from the coloured light machine and placed another next to the machine for me. Sara was in the next room with the children and was unable to participate. When everyone was seated, I turned off all the lights, so the room was in total darkness. I had deliberately chosen not to describe what I was going to do or what my audience would be experiencing. This wasn't an academic exercise but an experiential one.

I turned on the machine using the ruby red-light filter and said, "I'd like you to focus on the light and breathe deeply. If you feel comfortable to do so, say out loud what the colour reminds you of or how it makes you feel?"

"I don't like this ruby colour very much," Cathy shared with the group. "I work in a hospital and it reminds of blood that I see far too often."

One of Brian's friends said the colour made her feel sad, but she didn't know why.

"Whatever you are feeling is all right," I reassured the group, "just keep looking at the light and tell me if there is any change."

After a few minutes of silence, Brian spoke, "I don't think the colour bothers me as much as it did at the start. I'm getting used to it."

"I agree," said his friend. "I'm not feeling sad anymore." The others also agreed they were noticing some changes for the better in relation to the effect the ruby light was having on them.

"We tend to resonate at a certain vibration," I explained. "Colours also resonate at different frequencies. When we're not in balance, our natural vibration changes. At these times we might avoid certain colours, like red, for example. But when we keep looking at it, we can create an equilibrium."

The group nodded in understanding. A short while later they did not feel any effect from the red light. I took the red filter out of the coloured light machine and replaced it with an orange filter and then a yellow filter. Everyone agreed these colours made them feel comfortable. Next, I decided to press the strobing button and the light began to flicker at five flashes per second. This had an immediate impact.

"Please stop," came Brian's response. "I can't stand the flashing."

"Why?" I asked.

"It reminds me of the disco lights in the seventies. I never liked the seventies!"

Within a few minutes, Brian and the others calmed down amid the flashing lights. I increased the flash rate up to ten flashes per second, without causing further discomfort. At the end of an hour, I had used all fourteen colours and then shut the machine off. My guests were impressed with the experience and grateful

Chapter 9 — A Matter of Timing

for it. I thanked them for coming and giving me the opportunity to demonstrate the device I really believed in, but people still questioned.

The evening had been a success and now I was sure the vision workshop I had planned for Bendigo would also go well. But on Sunday night, I took a phone call from the organiser saying my vision workshop would have to be postponed due to low enrollment numbers. I was beginning to question my intuition after both the car raffle and this class had not worked out in the way I had felt they would.

I was losing confidence with the one consolation being the workshop had not been cancelled, only postponed. I did have to learn more patience and faith that opportunities would happen when the time is right and not when I wanted them to take place. I had to let things take their own course. That evening I meditated on this matter but did not feel any closer to identifying the reasons for the disappointments. However, I felt renewed in my longing to trust.

Sara suggested it might do me good to have her give me a healing session. She was using Reiki less and was relying on her intuition to tune into the person's needs. As Sara gave me a massage I drifted off to the sound of the soothing music.

The sound of Sara's voice brought me back. She spoke with a calm and reassuring voice. "I'm getting a message from your guides. They want you to know you are moving forward even though you may not be feeling that way. You have an important purpose, so trust and be patient. You should also watch your diet and avoid foods that may not agree with you."

I had not paid attention to nutrition in the past and less so recently. I was better with my food choices immediately after the operation, but with all the demands of the household and raising the children, Sara and I were more concerned about making sure we prepared food they liked rather than what we all should be eating. I knew the food I was eating wasn't satisfying

I had lost the desire for eating healthy foods. Now with Sara's and my guide's prompting I revived my interest. However, Sara and I disagreed about what was and was not nutritious and how we could achieve a balance. I had a nourishing breakfast the next day and decided to be more aware about my nutrition.

The final exam of my massage course was coming up in two weeks and while I was confident in the clinical part of the test, I was struggling with the theory. We were learning about bone structure and I had some difficulty recalling the anatomical names. Brian and I came together every evening to learn about the bones and the functions of the muscular system. We also had to learn about the skin, the nervous system and the endocrine system. I was interested in the endocrine system, especially the pituitary gland and the hormones it controls.

After hours of studying and going through mock exams, we felt well prepared. It had been years since I had studied so hard for an exam. Most of the assessment tasks for my previous post degree studies were either

Chapter 9 — A Matter of Timing

assignments or open book tests. I could not recall a time when I had required such intense memory work for an exam. I was definitely surprised by the three hundred and sixty-five questions on the test. As I worked through the questions, I predicted I might barely pass. I was feeling more confident about the practical exam scheduled for the next day. We were instructed to treat the client as we felt was most appropriate. I was good at using the various approaches to massage. My client had a spiritual disposition so rather than focusing on a clinical approach, I used an energy treatment.

I took a call from Kerrie a few days later, telling me I had not fulfilled all the requirements of the practical test. She took responsibility for instructing us to use whatever method we thought was necessary, but she had been wrong. She wanted us to use the methods she had taught us.

I called Magda that night and told her about my exam and the phone call from Kerrie. I explained I was reluctant to take the test again because I had done what was asked of me and felt it was not fair to change the instructions after the fact. Magda was sympathetic and suggested I could appeal. She recommended I do the test again because it would only take an hour and I had nothing to lose. "I don't think you'll use this therapy much anyway."

She had been the third person in as many weeks who had said that to me. I was concerned I had just spent a year on this course, and I hoped I would use it enough to recover the cost. But my instincts told me my friends were correct.

I decided to retake the test. Marcia, the woman who was my client for the first test came to my house for the exam. She was apologetic because it had not been my fault I had to do it again. She asked me to massage her left shoulder which had been troubling her. I completed the required preliminary examination and I found several sore points just above the scapula. I massaged the area for about a half an hour, and the area relaxed, but then I felt the middle of her back tighten. When I mentioned it, Marcia suggested the stress had shifted. This seemed to happen often when clinical massage was used, and it reaffirmed for me I had to use several forms of healing.

When I had finished Marcia asked me what I learned during the yearlong course.

"I've been asking myself the same question," I replied, "and some acquaintances have been telling me I may not use this therapy very much in the future. I think what I have learned is to combine the many modalities, including Reiki and Chiron healing, to really serve my patients. I should also incorporate spirituality on a level my clients can understand and feel comfortable with when I do use massage therapy. I don't understand why I needed to know so much about anatomy."

"Maybe you'll find out later," Marcia suggested. "After all, we don't know what the future will bring."

Our conversation convinced me I should continue to use massage at least for the near future. After talking to Brian about this, we decided to be proactive and not wait for people to come to us. He had heard of an

Chapter 9 — A Matter of Timing

alternative health fair being held regularly in Geelong and suggested we get a stall there and do some chair massage.

"Sounds like a good idea," I said. "Let's do it."

We organised a stall and Brian prepared our signs and created a brochure. We arrived at the fair in Geelong at seven o'clock in the morning on the following Saturday to set up our stall. We brought along some music, a variety of oils, an oil burner, the signs and brochures. The fair was not busy, so we did not have a lot of people stopping in for a massage. However, we did manage to make a small profit and learned from the experience.

That night, I set an intent for a dream to show me what I had learned. I dreamed another floor had been added onto the building where I worked. There were new accountants going into the building and up to the new floor, but I wasn't allowed to go up there. As I woke up, a thought crossed my mind. "The most important thing you can do is find your life's purpose."

I understood that to mean I was not going to get a job promotion at the accounting firm. I also took this message as suggesting massage itself was not my life's purpose, and I had to keep looking.

It was the first day of December, which was officially the first day of summer in Ballarat. I checked the mail and found a flyer about a ten-day workshop on vision and colour that was to be given by Andrew Whitecross. The seminar was to be held somewhere in far north Queensland.

I had mixed feelings about attending. I realised this would give my eye courses more credibility and I needed more formal training in this field. It occurred to me that vision workshops were more in line with what I had to do.

As quickly as my enthusiasm about the course began to grow, doubt crept in. The workshop was supposed to take place three thousand kilometers from where I lived. Where would I get the money to pay for the course? How would I get there? Where would I stay for ten days? I had been working four days a week, so we had very little left over from my paycheck and Sara was not earning very much at her part-time job. How could I justify another course when I had just finished paying for the massage course? While I was disappointed, I also realised it was only money that was holding me back.

I talked with Sara, who said it was my decision. If attending this workshop was very important to me then we would consider withdrawing some of the money tied up in long term investments, we had set aside for the children's education to pay for it. I was so grateful to her for trusting me, I decided to write to the bank about pulling out some of the money.

We also decided to take a weekend vacation, just the two of us. We hadn't been away for the whole year, while I was busy working and studying. I hoped to decide about enrolling in the course in Queensland by the end of the weekend. I could not come up with any good reasons not to go, as I would be on holidays during

Chapter 9 — *A Matter of Timing*

January when the program was being offered. I was booked for another MRI that month too, but that I could reschedule.

We went away for the weekend and had many thoughtful conversations. Sara asked me what I felt would be the benefits of this new course.

"Firstly," I started, "ten days of eating a vegetarian diet would be helpful for my digestive system. I guess I don't have to go, but my intuition tells me I should do this. I would learn valuable lessons from Andrew and in addition to that it looks like the type to program where I could discover a great deal about myself and perhaps help our relationship too." Sara was always very supportive. It made me feel loved.

I called Greg a few days later and told him I was particularly interested to go to Andrew's workshop, but I did not have the funds available to enroll immediately. That very afternoon, a letter came from the investment company to the effect they would release some of our money, but the process would take a few weeks. I was pleased and reserved my place straight away.

Magda offered to do some kinesiology about my attending this program. I decided to take her up on it. When I arrived at her home, she gave me a seat and handed me a glass of water. "Make sure you drink lots of water," she said as she began the session, "and be aware of everything that happens. You'll gain self-confidence and self-love, but it will be on your own terms."

One Vision

Christmas arrived and it was a time to give thanks for the past year. I had studied massage, Tai Chi, some kinesiology and had begun to understand numerology. Magda had suggested taking a full course in kinesiology, but I said I would do that sometime later. I had a positive feeling about Andrew Whitecross's ten-day workshop in Queensland. I was sure it would be a catalyst into a new area of growth for me and would put me on the right path. In preparation for the vegetarian diet at the seminar, I eliminated red meat and sugar from my diet. I was creating a mindset for what was to come. My path was becoming clearer.

Choice

Sara drove Jillian and me, to the Melbourne airport just before seven on Friday morning. Jillian was an acquaintance of ours and she had also signed up for the workshop. I hugged Sara and the children goodbye, and we walked into the terminal. At that time of day, the airport was bustling with people. When I looked at the monitors to check our flight, I noticed most of the flights were going to Sydney.

Jillian and I headed towards the check-in counter where, the attendant at the desk was very helpful, getting us organised for our journey. She was unable to seat us together as we had booked our flights and selected the seats separately. However, she arranged everything for our flight to Brisbane and the connecting flight to Townsville. She also reserved our return flights and assured us we would have seats together on that flight. After fifteen minutes, we handed over our luggage and were given our boarding passes. We boarded the plane thirty minutes later.

After taking off, I was glad to be alone so I could read the book I had brought with me. The flight attendant served refreshments and I read the chapter on the use and exchange of energy. 'All matter is made up of energy. As a result of this, it is possible to see the energetic patterns associated with physical objects. Scientists call this an electromagnetic field surrounding the object. Other people refer to it as an aura. Most commonly we refer to this field surrounding people, but it also exists around trees, plants and all forms of life. In order to see these energetic patterns, first of all, you need to be sufficiently open within yourself to the possibility that auras exist.'

I have seen auras. The most remarkable one I saw during a Chiron workshop with Michelle. After describing I saw auras as a shadowy glow around a person's head, I immediately noticed a deep green hue around Michelle that extended out to a half a metre around her body. Before I had time to tell her what I was seeing, a man called out, "I can see a deep green aura surrounding Michelle. It's a forest green colour." He had confirmed for me what I was seeing. Since then, I did not visibly see the colours, but felt the colour of auras. I had even seen auras surrounding a cluster of trees.

We had an hour wait in Brisbane before boarding our connecting flight to Townsville. The airports we were traveling through seemed similar and unpleasant. The heat and humidity of Brisbane were much higher than I

Chapter 10   Choice

was used to in Ballarat, so I chose to stay inside the air-conditioned building during our transit time.

I walked towards the lounge closest to the gate to Townsville and stopped to check the monitors for our flight details, when someone spoke to me. "Where are you heading?" asked a man in his mid-fifties with a woman standing by his side.

"Townsville," I replied.

"So are we," he said. "We flew up from Melbourne this morning. I'm Pat and this is my wife, Joy."

I introduced myself and asked them what they were doing in Queensland.

"We decided to spend our holidays traveling around far north Queensland. We are collecting a rental car in Townsville and driving up the coast to Cairns. What about yourself?"

"I'm on my way to Crystal Creek with my friend over there," I said, pointing to Jillian, who was a few feet away.

"We are driving through there today," said Joy. "You're welcome to join us for the drive."

Jillian and I had been considering how we were going to go the seventy kilometres from Townsville to Crystal Creek. We had thought about taking a bus, but that was so inconvenient. I was pleased we were given this opportunity.

"Thank you very much, that would be great," I said.

"It would save us from having to take a bus." The universe was looking after me.

Our drive went by quickly, with some interesting conversation. Pat and Joy were both Reiki channels. Pat told me as he stood next to me at the airport, he had a strong sense he should talk to me. On the flight he had been reading a book about following your intuition and was just starting the chapter on energy. We compared titles and were surprised to find we had been reading the same book. There are no coincidences. I was more convinced than ever that attending this workshop was where I was meant to be.

When we drove into Crystal Creek, we thanked Pat and Joy for their kindness and said goodbye. Outside of the car and the humidity struck me, and I realised we were certainly in the tropics. As we approached the living quarters we were greeted by a man and a woman who introduced themselves.

"Hi, I'm Dennis. Not much to look at is it?" said the man. Taking in the scenery around me, I saw rich tropical trees and shrubs. But the building was in poor condition, more like a summer camp bunker.

"I'm Joshua," I replied, shaking his hand. "I suppose the emphasis here is to focus on the learning not the physical accommodation," I said, comfortable with my observations. "Besides, I enjoy camping with my family, so I'm used to going without some creature comforts."

Jillian introduced herself to the woman whose name

Chapter 10 *Choice*

was Linda. She was Dennis' wife. She said they wanted to take some time away from their children and thought this course would be very interesting. After we settled in, I was told there was a creek about two hundred metres down the path, so I decided to go for a swim. I followed the track to a fork and considered which path to take. Remembering the chapter on energy I had been reading I saw one path appeared brighter than the other. I walked along that path until suddenly, the brightness disappeared. I looked to my right and noticed a narrower trail and it led directly to the creek where there were already several people swimming.

The energy around the creek was mesmerizing. It was surrounded by huge tropical trees that stood uninterrupted to the horizon then disappeared into the mountain tops. I stepped into the stream, immersing myself in the water and energy, sensing this was where I needed to be. Refreshed and feeling more whole than I had for a long time, I left the oasis and went back into conference centre. On the walk back I was bitten by a mosquito and I slapped it on my arm but then immediately realised I was disturbing the ecosystem so decided to avoid killing anything else during my stay.

When I walked in, Andrew was at the front of the room, deep in conversation with a small group. As I walked past him, he glanced at me and turned back to the group. I was disappointed. I had hoped he would give me more than a mere glance. Later when he began his session, he spoke of the need to be in the present moment. I suddenly became unsettled. I felt troubled being away from Sara and I was already missing her.

The next day we began with a meditation led by one of the other two facilitators. Ariel, a petite, Indian woman asked us to stand up for the meditation. We stood with our eyes closed and listened to the slow jazz music in the background. We swayed like trees to the music, but kept our feet grounded in Mother Earth. The experience left me feeling invigorated and ready for the day's activities.

When we introduced ourselves, I told the group I had come to this workshop because I owed it to myself. I am taking this time to relax, learn and perhaps transform my perspective, I explained. I took a chance and shared my disappointment about how I felt Andrew ignored me the day before. I recognised I had been caught up in the drama of the moment, determined now I would live in my truth and not get emotional. As soon as I said it, I no longer felt badly and could see the situation for what it was, that it was not about me.

"Joshua," Andrew spoke directly to me with a comforting tone. "You're a natural healer and will help hundreds of people with your gift. But to be truly effective, you should remember two things, first, be aware of, and control your anger; it will diminish over time, and second, use your voice to open out your vision. I see you are already doing some of that. You're not afraid to express your feelings and you're trusting what is true for you."

I appreciated Andrew's advice, but I still needed to learn how my voice related to how I perceived things. I was grateful to have the ten days to discover more about that. On the first day, the meals had been fairly ordinary, but they improved substantially on the second day. For the first time, I was enjoying mangoes and other tropical fruits. When the workshop ended for the day, I went back to the creek and relaxed in the water, feeling calm and centered. I thought back to the Essene period when Jesus walked the earth. The Essenes were a peaceful tribe who maintained their peaceful existence wherever they went. It felt like I had belonged to one of their communities.

The next morning, Dennis asked me to go for a run with him before breakfast. As I ran, I was thinking about my dream from the night before. In it I had gone to visit a friend, a very charismatic, but somewhat unorthodox priest whose superiors were trying to shut down his church. They had told him in order to keep the church open he had a week to accumulate twenty-two thousand dollars. I had suggested he go on television to make an appeal to a wider audience.

When analysing the dream, I reflected on the number twenty-two, which is my birth number. Using television to reach a larger audience was a message to me; I should look for a larger audience than was available to me now. As I ran along the path with Dennis, panic struck. Was the dream suggesting I ought to go on television? As a child, I had undergone years of speech therapy and still felt uncomfortable speaking in public.

I shared my dream and my fear with Dennis. He replied, "I have noticed sometimes you do speak quickly."

"I know I do. I think that's because my mind works

rapidly and I want to get all of my thoughts out before they're lost," I answered him.

"That's easy to remedy," Dennis said, reassuringly. "Just listen more carefully to yourself. You will find you'll naturally slow down." Every conversation these days led me further along my path. When I discovered another weakness or challenge, I just had to recognise it and go back to the beginning. Dennis was honest with me, and while I was feeling a little embarrassed about sharing my fears with him, I was grateful to learn how others saw me. Unsurprisingly Andrew's morning talk also focused on the need to start over. I was getting used to my ideas being validated.

A woman was dissatisfied with Andrew's lectures and finally spoke up.

"I'm not pleased with the way this event is going," she said. Her tone firm and annoyed. "I came here to learn how to improve my eyesight and we haven't done one eye exercise. I am also unhappy about my accommodation and I am not enjoying the meals. I am finding this workshop a complete waste of my time and I'm sure others feel the same way."

"How do you know what others are feeling?" Andrew asked.

"I've heard them talk," she said, "and I know their complaints have been ignored."

Some people nodded their heads in agreement. Some did not. I stayed centered throughout the exchange and disengaged from it. I did not want to get caught up in the emotion but listened from a neutral place.

After several others took the opportunity to express their views, Andrew explained what had occurred.

"Two matters have been raised. The first is about your expectations, and the second is you have chosen to group them under external matters such as accommodations and food. You have shrouded your feelings behind the group and concluded this is how everyone feels when they do not.

"This is precisely what I've been talking about this morning. If you are not satisfied with the seminar then I suggest you leave, and I will refund your money. But first, you should address the real reason you are unhappy and own it. Be in your truth and then decide if you wish to leave or are prepared to start again from a different perspective."

It seemed obvious to me she had some personal issues to deal with and her outburst was how she coped. The atmosphere in the room seemed to lighten up as a smile formed on her face. Her exchange with Andrew took on a different quality and they managed to resolve their differences. I was sitting next to Simon, one of the facilitators, as this disagreement had unfolded. Simon put his hand on my shoulder, and something heavy lifted from my heart. I mentioned this occurrence to the group during our break-out discussion and likened the sensation to walls coming down; walls I had built up for protection.

"I would like add something about my experience

with Joshua," said Simon. He was a short man who looked very relaxed in white shorts and a yellow golf shirt. "I've experienced healings before, when people have placed their hands on me, and I have felt their warmth. But when I placed my hand on Joshua's shoulder, I also felt his warmth. It was the first time I could generate energy from my hands."

Simon and I had bonded over this experience and we sat together at lunch. We both wanted to get the most out of this workshop. Andrew came over to our table and asked me, "How's Greg doing in Ballarat?"

"I think he's doing well, but I don't really see him very often. Why do you ask?" I said.

"I talked to him a few weeks ago," Andrew replied. "He seemed a bit envious that you were coming here to do this course, even though he undertook it a while ago. I think he anticipates you will accomplish more in the field of vision than he will."

I still could not see how that was going to happen and was trying to figure it out in my head. I thanked Andrew for his encouragement, and then walked down to the creek for another swim. After my swim I joined Dennis, Linda and Jillian for some ice cream.

We had found an old wooden general store, which sold everything from petrol to postage stamps. There was a selection of souvenirs, with a few locally made tea towels, utensils and toys. They also sold homemade tropical flavoured ice cream. I ordered a large mango and coconut ice cream cone and then went outside to the

Chapter 10   *Choice*

phone box to call Sara. I was so very happy to talk to her as I wanted to tell her what I had learned but could not seem to express it.

I had slept well and as I entered the conference room the next morning, I walked past some ants encircling a puddle of water. It appeared to me they did not have a worry in the world. Perhaps, I thought, I should try to do the same. The morning session was informative with Andrew giving a lecture on light and sunning. As I stared out the window observing the effect of sunlight on the trees, I suddenly stood up and announced, somewhat uneasily, "I am sorry, but I have to be honest. I cannot listen to you talking about the sun and its energy. I need to go out and enjoy the sunshine." I stood up and headed for the door.

"No need to apologise," Andrew called to my surprise. "We need more people to say what they think. Go out and enjoy yourself."

I left the building and walked towards the creek. I heard footsteps behind me and turned to find Sharon walking towards me on the path. She was in her late twenties with short, bleached hair. "That took courage to speak up. You did really well," she said excitedly. "I was thinking about doing the same thing, but I didn't have the nerve. After you left, I did the same."

"Would you like to go for a walk?" I asked, changing direction, and heading away from the creek.

"That's exactly what I'd like to do," Sharon said. "I know a great spot a little further down this path."

We walked in silence toward a towering, gum tree which must have been more than two hundred years old.

"Stop!" Sharon called to me. "Look up there!" She pointed to an intricate spider's web spread across two thick tree branches. I could see a large Huntsman spider sitting, waiting in the corner of the web. The air was cool under the trees.

"I am almost able to feel the fairies who live in these trees," Sharon said. "What do you think?"

"I'm not sure about the fairies," I replied. "But I do sense some wonderful energy here. I want to stay and watch. I think that huge spider is the gatekeeper."

"It does look like it's waiting for something," Sharon replied.

We watched the activities in the tree for a while and then headed back to the conference centre. On our walk, I became more conscious of every tree and rock we passed. We arrived at the campsite as lunch was being served. I was not very hungry, so I took a small plate of salad, and sat quietly away from everyone, enjoying being in nature.

Later, I did go back to the creek for a swim. I swam until I reached two large rocks, where I found Ariel and another woman sunbathing in the nude. I moved quickly and quietly around the rocks to be sure they did not see me and feel uncomfortable.

But I wasn't fast enough, and I heard Ariel call out, "Why don't you join us?" I could see I was the one feeling awkward. They were perfectly relaxed lying in the sun. I climbed up onto the rocks before I took off my shorts and spoke with them about my attitude towards my own sexuality.

Ariel explained her perspective; we are all connected to nature in our souls. She smiled and said, "Trees and animals don't cover themselves." With that, they both got up and dived into the water. I finally grasped why this place was called Crystal Creek as I admired how beautiful Ariel and the other woman's bodies were in the clear waters, surrounded by dense, green rainforest.

I thought about our discussion and dived into the water after the women. I wanted to asked Ariel what she thought were the boundaries of our sexuality. Flashbacks to the sixty's hippie movement, and what I perceived to be a time of free love flashed through my mind. I swam towards them and instinctively picked up two stones from the creek bed. I felt the energy of the stones. They emitted feelings of connection and a sense the boundaries we put on ourselves will find their natural place. We would not have to create any artificial lines of conduct.

By the time I reached Ariel, I had found the answer to my question. I explained to her I had to find the answers within myself first.

"By being honest with yourself, you'll discover what is or isn't appropriate for you," Ariel agreed and added the challenge was to stay centred. She said remaining clear was a continuous struggle for her and in her relationship with her husband, Simon. I told her the same applied to my wife Sara and me.

I spent the rest of the day communing with nature. I was grateful to Sara for supporting my decision to come to this seminar and during my meditation I felt a greater love for Sara and for myself than at any time before. I remembered the first time we met; I had sensed an instant connection with her and knew we were meant to be together.

Dennis, Sharon and I went for a run the next morning. Sharon found it difficult to keep up with the pace Dennis had set, so she slowed to a walk several times. I advised Dennis I would walk with Sharon so he could keep up his tempo. Sharon was glad to have me walk with her while she caught her breath.

We walked silently for some time at a steady pace just taking in our surroundings.

"What is the most significant wish you have for yourself?" Sharon asked breaking the silence and taking me by surprise.

The answer came easily. "I would like to be rid of my tumour," I said definitively.

"What do you mean by that?" she inquired.

"It's a little complicated," I said. "I have a tumour on my pituitary gland and in some ways, it's been a gift. When I was diagnosed with the tumour, it enabled me to explore new health options I would not have ever considered before. It has given me the freedom to think differently and do things in a different way." I could see

Chapter 10 — Choice

Sharon did not understand what I was trying to say, so I continued. "I am unsure if this approach is still working for me. Perhaps the tumour is still with me because I have a lot more to learn so I can help people heal. Ultimately, it is up to God, yet I do believe I can influence my future. I would prefer to grow and evolve as a person without the tumour."

Sharon said she comprehended what I had told her. She explained she was taking time to find her true self. She had decided to take time off work and go on an overseas trip. "My heart isn't in my work any longer," she added.

"I feel the same way," I said. "I would like to resign from my job by the end of this year. I still don't know how, but I know it's what I really want."

As we arrived at the camp, Sharon threw me a friendly smile, appreciating we were on a similar path. She said goodbye as she went to shower before the morning session. I went back to my room to change, with a pleasant thought in my head; I had shared honestly and freely, more about myself than I had ever done before, with Sharon, someone I hardly knew. She had an angelic personality for me.

At breakfast, I became aware of too many coincidences occurring in my life. I was enjoying a bowl of muesli when a large woman sat down beside me. She had on a colourful cotton dress. She and I had not spoken as yet but as she lifted her cutlery, I was awestruck by the ring on her right hand.

"I don't usually notice such things," I said. "But I'm very impressed by your beautiful ring."

She looked admiringly at her ring, which was a large pearl and smiled. "Yes, it's a special ring," she said, with an American accent. "I was diving near Miami back home in the United States. This pearl seemed to appear out of nowhere and lay there waiting for me to pick it up. I took it to a jeweler who told me it had come from the lost city of Atlantis, some fifteen thousand years ago. I had it set in this ring and have not taken it off since."

"I learned about Atlantis through the Edgar Cayce readings," I said, wondering if she knew about Edgar Cayce.

"Truly," she laughed. "I'm a member of the A.R.E. Do you know what that is?"

"It's the association studying the works of Cayce," I answered.

"Yes," she said. "I often go to the headquarters in Virginia Beach. They regularly have interesting speakers and offer courses there. You must come and visit."

I had a feeling I would be seeing her again, after this seminar, and told her as much. Meeting someone else who was part of the Cayce community, made me think about Ivan. I would have liked to be sharing this meeting with him and Sara. I had made numerous important connections at this seminar. Andrew's session later that day related to people sharing similar

Chapter 10 — Choice

experiences.

"Several of you have been going through some strange experiences here," he started. "But let me reassure you that is normal. You are becoming increasingly aware of yourselves. You are more receptive to viewing the big picture of your lives, rather than seeing it through a pinhole in a piece of card. You are becoming more alive."

"Andrew," Jillian, who was sitting next to me, interrupted, "I'm feeling as if everyone here has a message for me. It's as if each person came here just to support me." A few people in the room nodded in agreement.

"Thank you. We all came to this workshop for a reason, including me. We all came to learn and what you're feeling, Jillian, reflects what you need at this time in your life. Thank each person you meet for everything you receive from them. Do not look for the perfect answer or even the perfect question. Start anew each day. In fact, I invite you to start anew a hundred times a day."

I looked around and understood what he was saying. I had learned something from everyone, except one person. She was a woman in her fifties who reminded me of the nuns who had taught me at primary school. Later in the morning when we had a tea break, I took the opportunity to see what she might offer me. However, she was the one who came to me, put her arms around me and told me she thought I was excellent.

I was not uncomfortable with her show of affection and realised she was making me feel better about myself. Her honesty was refreshing, but I decided to be in my truth.

"I'm not great," I said. "I have my faults as we all do. Please remove your arms. I'm not sure this is appropriate." It felt right to express how I was feeling as I had with Ariel at the creek. The woman seemed embarrassed and quickly withdrew her arms. She explained she felt her actions were genuine and it was natural for her to express her emotions in such a way. As she turned to go outside, she added that by rejecting her embrace I must have issues with my own sexuality.

I learned another lesson in the afternoon when a young woman, Lisa, shared some personal stories about her teenage years. She told us she had been through her fair share of emotional turmoil and provided plenty of details, I truly did not want to hear. After some time, Simon who was unable to understand the significance of her anecdotes, interrupted her.

He stood up and addressed her, "Please get to the point, Lisa? Your story seems to be going on and on with no real substance. What is the problem?"

She looked at him with astonishment. "What I have been trying to say," she replied, sounding like a hurt child, "is my inner child is still searching for a way to express itself. It has been locked away like a bird in a cage."

"That's just New Age bullshit," Simon confronted

her, and raised the conversation to another level. "I'm not denying the inner child exists. What I am hearing is you are hiding your true feelings in this long saga you are telling us, and you are using language that is not your own. If you are angry, say so. Don't try to explain it away."

Tears ran down her face as she lashed out at Simon. "I'm really pissed off," she shouted. "I've always had to do everything myself. No one was ever there for me." In that moment, I heard myself telling my own story based totally on my tumour. I decided I no longer had to include details of my tumour when I told people my story. I could start again.

Following the confrontation between Simon and Lisa, my emotions were heightened, so I decided a swim in the creek would help me to relax. I was discovering the importance of water for me. I was learning from the water when I swam and the rocks when I held them in my hands.

As I reached the bank, I was captivated by the torrent of water racing between the two large boulders where I occasionally sunbathed. The current was effortless and was not deterred by the obstacles in its way. I made a decision standing there watching the water. I chose to go with the flow, to stop swimming against the tide and driving my way forward.

As I remained there a man in a canoe paddled into my view and climbed out. He looked over to me and asked if I wanted to borrow it. I didn't know him and was surprised by his generosity. I accepted his offer and scrambled into the canoe. I paddled to the rocks and allowed the water to carry me down stream. My spirits lifted and I thoroughly enjoyed the trip, paddling gently every now and then to avoid the thick branches in my path.

Later when I met up with Andrew, I described what had happened to me and how I felt so connected to the creek. "When you live in the moment, things happen Joshua and, forgive the pun, just jump in."

In the evening I decided to jump in feet first and told Sharon, she seemed to be an angel to me.

"I'm glad you told me," she smiled sweetly, "because I've felt so comfortable with you. You helped me recognise how I feel about myself. We seem so innocent, almost child-like."

I had not thought of myself as being innocent and I was not sure what she meant by that, but it didn't seem necessary to ask her.

The next day, I talked to Simon about what had happened to me during the past six days. "I have learned," I said, "that being aware means knowing who you are as well as understanding others. It is about the details of the day, like picking up towels and doing the laundry. Being present in everything we do. Sara will be pleased when I start to do that more often," I added with a smile.

"It's also about not taking the spiritual path too seriously. It is about having fun and enjoying art and music. My passion is music. I encourage you to find

Chapter 10   Choice

yours," Simon affirmed.

I was starting to feel closer to Simon. Andrew seemed to be distancing himself from the group and was more guarded. Simon, on the other hand said what he felt without any self-consciousness. He was a co-leader but behaved more like one of the participants. I had been impressed by the way he dealt with Lisa. He was hard on her but also showed compassion.

"How do you define enlightenment?" I asked, attempting to go deeper.

Simon seemed pleased to answer, "To me, enlightenment is not something we acquire. It's a lifelong process you can choose to work towards or not. We make choices every moment about the way we live our lives and what's important to us."

"And what about Karma?" I asked. "Isn't what we do in the present determined by our past actions?"

"For sure," said Simon. "They are lessons we choose for ourselves." He considered his words before he continued, "I believe we look to the future and not the past. We can determine our future regardless of the mistakes of our past. It is the choices and decisions we make now that create the person we become. What do you want your future to be?"

"In terms of work," I said, "I would like to quit my accounting practice and help people with their vision, both their eyesight and insight. I want to help people discover and reach their full potential."

One Vision

The cook interrupted us to let me know I had a phone call. I hugged Simon and went to the phone. It was Sara calling to hear about how I was getting along. I brought her up to date since our last conversation. It felt wonderful sharing my thoughts with her. "Everything here has been amazing, but I really miss you and I'm ready to come home."

"It's just a few more days, and you're gaining so much from the workshop. Stay and you will have even more to tell me when you get home," she said, and added, "I have some good news for you. I took a call from Bendigo. You can go ahead with your workshop as they now have enough people signed up. I had them reserve the first weekend in March, if that date is all right with you?"

"That's brilliant, Sara. I had just finished telling someone here what I really wanted to do was run the vision workshops. Isn't that amazing?" I was thrilled.

Such great news. My future was taking shape. We continued to talk for a while, as she told me about some of her coincidences. We were having similar experiences even though she was three thousand kilometres away.

The Journey

"I have a strong voice," I repeated to myself each day, upon waking. Every day I was gaining a deeper perspective of who I was and what I had to do. Each night I would look ahead to a new and more enlightening day. Each day of the workshop built on the previous day; I felt as if I was learning a new language and my voice was becoming clearer.

I had decided not to go for a run with our group, this morning. I was spending more and more time away from the group. I was feeling detached from the others who appeared to be connecting at a deeper level during the social activities. I did not understand the reason for my remoteness.

I walked to the kitchen mindful of each step. The slower I walked, the more aware I was of every stride. I was fully conscious of the rising sun and the colours of the trees. Although the walk took me ten minutes, time seemed to have stood still.

It was early when I found myself alone in the kitchen, so I poured myself a bowl of cereal and sat down at a carefully set table to eat. I put my hand on the cereal bowl and invited God to make the food I was about to eat enjoyable and agree with me. As I took each spoonful, I focused my attention on it and thought about everything I had learned about eating well. I had received some valuable advice regarding food; eat your food slowly, don't talk with your mouth full and don't leave the table until you're finished. I now understood the truth behind each statement.

I had learned a great deal about nutrition and understood if you are mindful, you can eat anything as long as you eat in balance. I pushed the bowl away from me when I had finished eating and put my elbows on the table to do some palming. I said a prayer for the good food I had eaten.

I took my hands from my eyes, slowly stood up and took my dishes to the sink. I washed my utensils and put them away. Feeling calm, I walked into the conference room. I looked around at the thirty chairs scattered around the room and noticed someone sitting at the far end of the room. I hardly recognised Brendan because he had shaved off his beard. He looked much younger than when I had seen him just a day ago.

Brendan was sitting cross-legged on the floor with his eyes closed and did not notice me. I did not want to disturb him. I stood in the doorway, closed my eyes, and

Chapter 11 — The Journey

breathed into my abdomen. The word 'trust' came to mind as I stood their questioning what I should do next. Slowly, I stepped forward a few inches with my right foot and started to sway to an internal rhythm.

The room felt fresh and I sensed I was there to learn something about trusting. We had done a number of walking meditations to music. I kept opening my eyes to make sure I did not bump into anything or anyone. I continued to open my eyes in order to feel in control of my environment. Now I knew I had to trust by keeping my eyes shut. I took another step and brought my left foot next to my right one, as I edged further into the room with my eyes closed.

When I sensed I had reached the first chair, I stopped. I was worried about bumping into the chair. Was Brendan watching me pick my way around the room? Why was he there? Why was I?

I felt I needed to open my eyes to check if my path was safe when I remembered it had been Brendan who told me I had to step out to get what I wanted. It was Brendon I had spoken to about changing careers and moving forward. He had said, "If you truly believe you know where you want to go, you will get there."

I decided to continue. This was my chance to move forward. I took one large stride forward and nothing happened. I took several more paces before my hand brushed against a chair as I passed by it. I had sensed the chair's presence even before I touched it. I continued for several minutes with my eyes closed and walked by a few chairs without my way being blocked. I walked faster and faster and when I finally opened my eyes, I found I had reached the middle of the room.

I felt centred and positive. As I let these feelings flow over me, I was reminded of the time when I had studied Tai Chi. The movements were performed with a precise flowing style. I could not accomplish them then but now feeling as I did, I was sure I could be successful.

I looked across the room and saw Brendan smiling at me. We didn't say a word and then I left. We both knew I had succeeded in trusting myself and the future was now open to unlimited possibilities.

During the day I was conscious of every little detail, from brushing my teeth to making my bed. I had engaging discussions with Simon and Ariel during the morning, both generating new insights for me. I felt a strong connection to them both. There was nothing sexual in the attraction I felt for them but something more transcendent. It was as if their energy surrounded me. I could hear their words and anticipate their actions before they occurred.

Amazingly the same considerations spread to the rest of the group. I had feelings of connectedness with others where exchanges were instinctive. I kept thanking people to the point where they were becoming annoyed.

Dennis implored me to stop thanking everyone and to accept the feeling of connectedness. "Just enjoy the moment and accept it," I would tell myself. Dennis was right. I felt aligned with the people around me and with the universe. Continually thanking people was

Chapter 11 — The Journey

disrupting the flow of the moment. I considered my anxiety about these new feelings to be natural. As I did on most mornings, I went for a jog. So much had happened and I needed some alone time. I focused on slowing my breathing and ran oblivious to my surroundings. I expected to find another beach further along the creek but instead came upon another path between the track I was on and the creek. It had the same glow as the path I had taken down to the creek on my first day.

I didn't consider the dangers of taking an unfamiliar path but turned onto it and started walking. I found myself in an area where the stream was wilder and was possibly inhabited by snakes and crocodiles. When I reached the bank, I scanned the area upstream. I saw someone standing on the rocks on the other side. My shoes were already wet, so I unconsciously decided to swim across. The person standing on the rock appeared to be glowing. When I arrived on the other side, I could see more clearly the likeness on the rock was a woman and she appeared to be waiting for me. As I moved closer, the figure disappeared. By the time I had reached the rocks, the form had moved further along the stream.

I followed the image upstream, swimming some of the way, and then walking, trying to reach her, but each time I would get closer the figure would move. I imagined she was an angel and wondered why I was being challenged to go to her. I climbed onto the largest rock in the middle of the creek and searched for her as far as my eyes could see. The angel was gone, and I felt totally alone. Was I feeling so detached because I felt superior to the others or was it because I really wanted to be at home with Sara, sharing all I had gained from this experience with her? I stood up straight and lifted my face to the sky and shouted at the top of my voice, "I'm standing on my own pedestal," establishing I was in control of my future.

I felt free and ready to cross my own the winning line. There was no competition. We were all here to learn, to walk a personal path and keep moving forward. I stepped onto another rock and although it was the same as all the others, I felt it was the only one above water. I closed my eyes and I felt my thoughts were suspended in space. I heard the current and the air flowed through me. I took a step and my left foot came to rest on another rock. I recalled how I had walked around the conference room with my eyes closed and had not bumped into anything. Again, I cleared my mind and I took one step after another. I crossed the river before I opened my eyes and checked my position. Instantly, I fell into the water.

I climbed back onto a nearby rock and saw there were not enough rocks for me to walk back to the other side. Again, when I looked down, I fell into the water. I decided to try to make it to the other side with my eyes open and looking straight ahead. The trees, the sky and the clouds, all seemed to be supporting me in my quest. I stepped out and my foot landed on what felt like solid ground. Every step I took was bolstered and I walked freely to the middle of the creek.

I was filled with joy because I had trusted. I dived into the water and swam back to the campsite. I no

Chapter 11 — The Journey

longer fought my way upstream but almost floated down the creek. I could clearly see colourful pebbles lining the bottom of the creek in intricate configurations. I splashed down the rapids and felt a child-like fascination with my surroundings. I would stay underwater for longer and longer periods of time and then rise the surface to take in some air. It was a magical swim and when I arrived back at the camp, I went straight to my room to write down everything I experienced so I could share it with Sara.

As the events at the creek flashed before me, I felt incapable of writing. What could I say? The effect was more profound than the actual events and I could not put it into words.

I looked down at the paper where I had written 'An Adventure' at the top of my page and scribbled random words below it. I read; there is a river, go with the flow, and watch as the ripples expand. Each phrase conjured up another image and an added sensation. I felt connected to the creek, and through it, to the Universe.

There was nothing more to write, so left my room and walked towards the conference room where I found Andrew in conversation with a few people. I sat on a chair nearby and they stopped talking. Andrew asked, "Did you enjoy your swim?"

I realised I was still in my wet clothes. "Yes, thanks," I said with a grin.

The group turned back as Andrew finished talking to me. They were discussing the changes they had experienced during the last few days. Andrew had filled the white board with notes, and I turned my attention towards it.

'There is a transition period as we move from our old life to the new. Our emotional numbness transforms into the place where peace, love and freedom reside. Sometimes we experience grief as our lives will never be the same.'

My life had changed down at the creek. I had learned through my experience life is much easier if you go with the flow. The water flowed around the rocks effortlessly as it moved down the stream. The rocks became smooth as they allowed the water to pass.

I listened as the group described their experiences. One person explained he did not feel like something had died, rather that something was reborn, and he felt more alive.

Afterwards, the group went for a swim. It felt good to be part of the group as we took hold of a rope and one by one jumped into the creek. I had not played with a group like this for many years and I was thoroughly enjoying myself. In the evening we found a variety of musical instruments and accompanied an African jazz recording. We played, clapped and danced to the pure rhythm.

Back in my room I collapsed on my bed exhausted. My mind was working overtime, yet I felt relaxed, and planned to sleep in the next day to prepare for the day's activities. But when morning came, a mosquito

Chapter 11   *The Journey*

disturbed my sleep and woke me early. I was only half awake, but I decided to ask the mosquito to land on my right index finger, which it did. I got up and opened the door and asked it to fly away. Again, it did just that. -

I was getting excited anticipating the day. I dressed and walked around the campsite as if I had never seen it before. Each tree, each blade of grass seemed to offer something to me, some spark of wisdom. I walked methodically and found myself at the front door of the complex. There was a plaque on the door with the camp's name and a poem. The poem, 'Footprints', is one I had read dozens of times, but now, as I read it slowly and out loud, I knew I understood it for the first time.

'A man had a dream. He dreamed he was walking along the beach with the Lord. Across the sky flashed scenes from his life. In each scene, he noticed two sets of footprints in the sand; one belonging to him, and one belonging to the Lord. When the last scene of his life flashed before him, he looked back at the footprints in the sand. He noticed that many times along the path of his life there was only one set of footprints. He also noticed that it happened at the very lowest and saddest times in his life.

'This really bothered him, and he questioned the Lord about it. "Lord, you said that once I decided to follow you, you'd walk with me all the way. But I have noticed during the most troubled times in my life, there is only one set of footprints. I don't understand why you'd leave me when I needed you most."

One Vision

'The Lord replied, "My precious, precious child, I love you and I would never leave you. During your times of trial and suffering, when you see only one set of footprints, it was then that I carried you."'

I too have asked Jesus for his help and received it. Not necessarily the help I had asked for, but perhaps, the help I needed. I considered the poem as I continued my walk, when I heard someone call out, "Peace, brother."

I noticed Andrew coming towards me. "How are you this morning?" he asked.

"I'm not sure," I replied. "I'm not sure whether things are happening to me or if I'm dreaming them. I'm not differentiating between dreaming and what I believe to be real."

Andrew smiled reassuringly, "I'm about to begin the day and it would be good to see you inside." We walked back to the conference centre and found everyone already seated.

Andrew went up to the front of the room and began to talk about the transition between the old life and the new, but I found I was unable to stay focused on what he was saying. I decided I needed to go back to the creek and connect with the water. I stood, walked out of the room and headed down the path. I wasn't sure if anyone saw me leave. On my way down to the creek, I met Simon, who was walking back towards the camp.

"Where are you going?" he asked as he reached me.

"For a swim," I managed to mutter.

Chapter 11 *The Journey*

"Why don't you do that later," Simon suggested, "and come back with me. It's almost morning-tea time."

I shrugged and continued down the path. When I reached the bank, I found an old, inflated tyre tube on a table. I picked it up, and jumped into the water with it, letting the current take me down stream. I sat in the centre of the tyre, and the rapids took me to a part of the creek I had not previously explored.

When I thought of going back to camp, I noticed the current was very still. I watched the water curve around a cluster of trees into an embankment covered by stones. I looked back upstream and saw an identical picture in my mind. The same curved bend, the same trees, and the same stones along the embankment. Both paths appeared to be identical as if it didn't matter which way I went.

I did not feel like forcing my way back upstream, so I continued to float with the current. Occasionally I dived into the water to escape from the sun's heat. A little later on, I stopped and focused on the light coming from the other side of the creek. The picture was one I had seen in my mind before. I paddled to the edge of the water, climbed onto the bank and threw the tyre into the creek. -

I clambered to the top of the bank and found a row of mango trees. There was a large farmhouse and shed at the end of the orchard. The view before me looked like paradise; a creek flowing with crystal clear water, rich, green grass, tree-covered mountains, and a perfect blue sky. As I approached the farmhouse, a man came bursting out of the door, carrying a rifle, yelling at me to get off his property. I panicked, turned back the way I came and walked back into the water. I began to swim upstream, staying in the water for most of the day. I came across some ropes floating in the creek. I held onto one and allowed the current to take me downstream. Then I turned against the flow to make my way back upstream again. I was hoping someone would join me in what felt like a game; but no one came. The feeling of aloneness gripped me more and more until it turned to fear.

I made my way out of the creek and began to wander down a dirt track. I was feeling truly alone. I noticed there was garbage lying all over the ground, damaging the natural beauty of the area. I found an old cloth bag and tied it around my waist. I started to fill it with bits of paper and cans until it was full. Then I collected more rubbish until my arms were unable to hold anymore. Even though I had picked up all that I had; it did not seem to make a difference. It occurred to me it was time for me to get rid of my own garbage.

I could not carry the rubbish any longer, so I bent down to put it into a pile at the side of the track. As I bent down, I noticed a set of footprints that ended where I did. I remembered the words from the poem, and I felt safe in my solitude.

The afternoon sun continued to beat down on me. I stepped into the water to cool down and instinctively scooped up some mud and rubbed it over my body for protection from the sun. I was careful to cover myself all over. The next several hours became a blur. I realised I had not eaten for more than twenty-four hours, so I

Chapter 11   *The Journey*

climbed out of the creek and continued down the track, picking berries from the bushes as I went. I kept walking for hours.

When night came, I burrowed myself into a hollow beneath some mango trees, where the earth was moist and warm. I lay there unaware of where I was or where I was going. I tried to sleep but could not because of the buzzing sound of mosquitoes. Then the rain came.

The next thing I remember I was standing in an open field in the middle of the night. I couldn't tell if I was awake or dreaming. Twelve angels appeared to my left in two rows as if a trial was about to begin. A shadowy outline resembling Sara appeared on my right. Some sort of proceeding was taking place, but I could not hear anything. I could only feel. I felt I needed to let Sara go, but with unconditional love. Then came the words I had to release Sara from her marriage vows. To do this I had to throw away my wedding ring. By doing this I could share Sara's spirit. "I love you, unconditionally," I shouted and threw the ring into the air.

Now, I could offer myself to Sara without any attachments. With all bonds broken she was free to choose; to stay or to leave. The angels gestured for me to step forward, and as I took a long step, they began to sing like a choir. "Come home with us, you are part of us. You can come home."

I felt infinite peace and love, but Sara was still standing on my right. "I would prefer to stay with Sara," I said. "I love her and want to share my life with her. Let me stay with Sara."

As I spoke those words, the angels began to fade, and were moving further and further away from me. I reached out towards their fading image, trying hard to hold on to the feeling of peace. When the angels had disappeared, I turned towards Sara who was waiting for me.

"Thank you, Joshua," she said. "I love you unconditionally, too." With that, her image also disappeared, although her love stayed with me as I closed my eyes.

I do not know if hours or moments had passed. I was dancing surrounded by the sound of beautiful music. When I stopped dancing, I could not speak. I danced again and stopped. Now, I had lost my sense of hearing. All the noises, the buzzing of mosquitoes, the sounds of nature, were gone. There was nothing but silence. Hysterically, I continued dancing and stopping. Each time I stopped, I lost another sense: smell, touch, and finally my sight. I stood perfectly still, only breathing and feeling my heart beating. Then my breathing stopped, and my heart began to slow down. I surrendered myself to God and there was total silence, a feeling impossible to describe. All was still. My mind was quiet. From somewhere within me, I saw a tiny glow. In the haze of total nothingness, there was a glow radiating from within me. I knew it was my essence, my spirit.

Slowly, through the grace of God, my heart started to beat again and then I drew a breath. Each sense came back in the same order in which it had left, but it was different. I had to relearn to breathe, to see, to touch and for my heart to beat. It was as if I were operating from a different place with a different point of reference, which I could only describe as love. I was functioning with my heart and not my mind.

Morning came and I wandered through a field of sugarcane until I came across what looked like an American Indian teepee. It was raining, so I entered the tepee, which was dry inside. I began searching for what I needed to learn; looking for a message inside. I crawled along the ground hoping to make some sense of what was happening but didn't find anything.

I heard birds outside just above me, screeching. I thought I heard them calling to me, so I listened. There were no right or wrong paths for me to take. I was free to choose whichever way I wanted to go. I wanted to go home.

I left the teepee and followed another track I had not noticed before. It led me to the same farmhouse I had found near the mango orchard. The man came out of the house shouting obscenities at me to leave again. "I love you," I told him not fully aware of what I said or the outcome it would have.

His attitude immediately changed. "What's wrong?" he asked in a calm, amiable voice.

"I think I'm lost," I said. "Can you tell me how to get back to the camp at Crystal Creek?"

He came over and pointed to yet another track. "But you'd better take these," he said, and handed me a pair of blue shorts that were hanging on a clothesline. "You

One Vision

don't want to be walking around just wearing an old paper bag." I thanked him for his kindness and put on the shorts. My response to him had made a big difference to how he responded to me. We had both benefited from our meeting.

I walked down the track he had pointed out to me, but I still felt lost. I didn't know where I was going. I sat down on the path and picked up lumps of dirt, letting it fall back through my fingers to the ground. As a small pile started forming on the ground, I noticed the pile was changing into the shape of a golden goblet. I tried to pick the goblet up in my right hand, but it just turned into another pile of soil.

I tried once more to grasp the goblet, but I could not, so I stood up. I walked further along the trail and saw the shop where we had gone for ice cream a few days ago. I went over to the store and up to the counter. The woman behind the counter stared at me as I came closer, sunburned, covered in mosquito bites, and wearing only the pair of blue shorts.

"I'd like some ice cream," I managed to get out. "I left my money at the camp, so I'll have to pay for it later."

"I don't normally do this," she said. "But I think I can make an exception just this once." I pointed to the tub of mango ice cream and she gave me a single scoop. As I was standing there slowly licking the ice cream, an older man came out from behind the shop.

"You must be the man everyone is searching for," he

Chapter 11 — *The Journey*

said, noticing the state I was in. "Are you all right?"

"I'd appreciate a lift back to the camp, please," I replied, doing my best to sound courteous. "I'm feeling a bit tired."

"Sit down over here," he suggested, escorting me to a chair near the window. "I'll call the police to let them know you're here."

I didn't understand why he was calling the police when I just wanted to get back home. I sat and was finishing eating my ice cream when two policemen and Ariel came into the shop.

"How are you?" Ariel asked, putting her arms around me.

"How did you get here?" the older policeman asked me, before I could answer the first question. "We've been looking for you all night."

"Thank you," I said to the policeman. "I didn't know anyone was looking for me. I managed to find my way back here."

"I think we need to get you to a hospital," he continued, "to make sure you are all right."

"I'd like to go back to the campsite. I think I'll be going home today," I said, without any hesitation.

Ariel assured the policemen she would take care of me and they took us both back to the camp. I thanked the policemen and Ariel took me to my room. "We need to do something about your sunburn," she said, suggesting a shower might help. I managed to get myself into the shower, and as I was coming out, I found two ambulance officers in my room. They examined me to ensure I was healthy. They wanted to take me to the hospital for observation, but I declined their request and agreed to sign a refusal form.

Some people from our group checked in on me and brought me fruit to eat and creams to soothe my body. In my altered state, I knew who was coming to see me and why they were coming before they entered the room. As each person came in, I thanked them for what they had taught me during the session and would offer to them just what they needed too, without them having to ask. They, in turn, gave me what I needed, as it came into my mind.

When Sharon came in, I explained to her how strange I felt.

"Do not rush," she said. "It will take some time for you to adjust to your new way of life. Allow yourself to get better first."

"What's happened to me?" I asked, not knowing how to phrase the question.

"By the sounds of it," Sharon said calmly, "you've gone traveling into a higher dimension. Why didn't you tell someone you were going?"

"I didn't know I was," I answered. "It's as if I didn't have a choice."

"On a higher level, you probably didn't," Sharon

Chapter 11 — The Journey

commented. "But anyway, for now, I think you need to just lie there and rest."

"What about Sara?" I asked. "Does she know I'm safe?"

"She was notified by the police that you were missing last night, and they have contacted her again this morning to let her know we have you back with us. But Joshua, you need to rest your body." With that, she left my room, and I dozed off.

I was half-awake and found myself alone in the room. Although I was still drowsy from my nap, I had complete clarity something had happened to me while I was missing from camp. As I reflected on the events, a light breeze blew through my mind and I could not remember anything. After this happened several times, I understood my memories were being hidden from me. A voice inside my head was saying so much had occurred it would be too difficult for me to cope with it all at once, and most would have to be veiled until later when I was ready.

I tried to negotiate, to retain some of my experiences, before the breeze took away another one. I tried to hold on to my pitch perfect singing voice. "You'll have to work on that," came the whisper, as I felt my singing voice disappearing. But the memory of my voice remained.

I could feel Andrew nearby just before he appeared in the doorway of my room. He entered the room and stood next to my bed. "Please join us for the last session," he proposed. "I think it would be beneficial for the group if you did."

"No," I said intuitively. "I don't want to be put on display. I've spoken with each person and completed what I needed to do with them."

"What do you mean?" Andrew said, somewhat taken back by what I had said.

"You gave me the gift of finding myself and I thank you for that," I said. "My gift to you is to encourage you to believe in spirit more and to trust your angels and guides. They have been with you on your journey. Be grateful for them."

"How dare you instruct me about what I need to know," he said indignantly. "I think you need to be a little less arrogant."

My response was calm.

"I'm sorry for the awkward way I expressed this. I am not used to speaking from the heart and telling people what I know to be true. I genuinely feel I have offered you advice I know is a gift."

He turned and walked out of my room. He responded in a manner he believed to be his truth, and I had to allow him that.

A minibus arrived to take some of us to the airport. I said my goodbyes and thanked those members of the group who were not traveling with me before I clambered onto the bus holding the pillow I had brought along. My suitcase had been put into a trailer behind the

Chapter 11 *The Journey*

bus with the others. The atmosphere on the bus was vibrant with people sharing all they had learned as we made our way to Townsville. Sharon and Jillian were absorbed in conversation behind me.

Every now and then, Sharon would gently place her hand on my shoulder and asked if I was all right.

"I'm okay," I would reply, not fully aware of the goings on around me. After she had asked about my well-being a few times, I told her, "I think my eyesight is better than ever now. I have total clarity when I look at you or at the trees along the roadside." I was so pleased looking around.

When we reached the airport, I took some money out of my wallet to pay for my part of the bill. Jillian explained she had my plane ticket and would look after everything for me, so I could just sit and rest. There were eight of us at a restaurant table inside the airport and someone had ordered a chocolate cake to share. When it appeared at the table, I was offered a piece. When I took a bite, I felt weighed down.

"Very grounding, isn't it?" Jillian said to me with a big smile.

"Certainly is," I replied, trying to understand what was happening to me.

I went to use the bathroom before we boarded the plane, and as I was heading back to the waiting area, I heard my name being called over the public announcement system. I went to the information desk and introduced myself.

"Those people would like to speak to you," the airline attendant replied.

I walked across to where the two people were waiting. One of them introduced herself and explained she was a reporter for the 'Townsville Gazette.' Her partner was a photographer.

"May I ask you a few questions about what happened to you, Mr. Winter?" she inquired. "Do you know what happened, Joshua?"

The memory of drifting down the creek floated to the surface of my mind as her partner took a picture. The next moment I had forgotten everything.

"I don't remember," I said as my memory went blank as it had done previously in my room.

"Where did you sleep last night?" she asked. Again, the thought of burrowing under the mango trees appeared and as the photographer's flashlight flickered in front of my eyes, the memory disappeared.

"I don't know," I replied again.

She continued to ask more questions but with each query and camera flash, I could not remember any detail I could share with her. Finally, she stopped asking and finished the interview with, "Thank you, that's all we need." I rejoined the others just as the flight was called.

When the plane touched down in Melbourne several hours later, I knew my life would never be the same. My legs had become stiff from sitting for so long and Jillian helped me walk along the gangway. Ivan and Magda were there to meet us and were so happy to see me alive, they both tightly hugged me.

"We didn't know what had happened to you," Magda said. "It's so good to see you."

I felt unbalanced and found it difficult to walk to their car. Once I was seated in the back seat, I slept all the way back to Ballarat. I arrived home around midnight and as I opened the door, I heard Sara call my name as she came out of the bedroom.

"Welcome home," she said, tears glistening in her eyes.

One Vision

Expectancy

"Thank you, God," I prayed as I woke up in the morning. "Thank you for giving me the chance to start again. I pray I will not fill my new stage with old costumes. I am learning to be a co-creator of my life and not a follower."

"How are you feeling?" Sara asked when she noticed I was awake.

"Vulnerable," I replied. "I feel as though I've just been put through a wringer."

"You were shaking all night," Sara uttered. "I'll make an appointment with the doctor for you this morning."

Sara went out to the kitchen to call the doctor and to make me breakfast. I felt different with every breath, and I would catch myself holding my breath for no apparent reason.

Alone in our room, I examined my body. I was sunburned, completely covered in mosquito bites, and I had several abrasions on my arms and legs. As I applied some more cream to my body, it occurred to me, it could have been a lot worse, had I not had the protection of my spirits and guides.

I went to see my doctor who was more concerned with making my body healthy again, than I was.

"From what you have told me, you had an interesting time while you were missing," he said. "But my priority is to help you heal your body. You could have the Ross River Virus or a whole host of other diseases that are carried by mosquitos. I also want to examine your tumour for changes."

He took several vials of blood, and feeling exhausted and weak, I went home and slept until Ivan and Magda came by to see me.

"How is he?" I heard Magda ask Sara.

"Still disorientated," Sara said. "Please come in. He's just waking up."

Ivan brought a cup of chamomile tea into the bedroom for me. He placed it on the bedside table and sat next to me. "Still with us?" he asked smiling.

I sat up and took a sip of the tea and thought about what I wanted to say to Ivan. "The trip home was strange," I started. "I saw large hot houses everywhere, on fields as big as football fields. They were shaped like

Chapter 12 — Expectancy

domes. I was sure they must be small communities who were self-sufficient and growing their own food."

"You may have had a vision of the future," Ivan suggested. "I also believe that's how we will be growing our food in the years to come, in order to get the full benefit of the nutrients, and to eliminate the need for preservatives and putting chemicals into our foods. Naturally grown, organic foods resonate better with our vibration."

"What do you mean by that?" I asked.

Ivan was so excited talking about these ideas with me, he did not fully explain himself. "What I mean to say is," he continued, "food affects everything in our life; from how we perform physically to our emotional wellbeing. Have you noticed it is difficult to meditate after a large meal of fried chicken? Eating light, natural foods provides a better source of energy and we can digest them more easily. However, most people find it very difficult to break bad food habits. When they do change their diet, they will feel bad at first, but as their body adjusts and is cleansed, then they feel much better. It's recommended we start a vegetarian diet slowly to allow our bodies time to adjust."

"Yes, I understand," I said. "For me, it was wonderful to see people growing their own food in small communities and sharing everything."

"Community living makes a lot of sense," Ivan agreed. "It does seem strange to me, to be living next to people we never see or talk to, let alone share with them the food we produce. Imagine if everyone on a street owned one lawn mower and shared it among themselves. Then they could buy the best equipment to maintain their lawns. They might even be willing to help when someone gets sick and is not able to do the work for themselves. Everyone would benefit."

"If only people were less interested in accumulating possessions, they could focus on more important issues," I said. "There are a lot of factors to consider before you can do this, but you have to start somewhere. So, you start with whatever item is most needed today and, over time, build up the infrastructure every street or community needs to become fully self-sufficient. When someone leaves, their share in the equipment could be bought by the group and then the new homeowner can purchase it, because in all likelihood, they're coming from a similar street or community. This allows them to immediately become a responsible member of the new street or community."

"You could also give your excess away," I suggested. "If we all gave away the items we no longer needed, they would benefit someone else, and again, everyone would be better off."

"I hear what you are saying," said Ivan. "However, people still see owning things as important. It seems to define who they are or how successful they are. But I can see changes happening or needing to happen. Imagine what would happen if large insurance companies went broke because of one or two disasters, like an earthquake in Los Angeles. It would have a massive effect on the economy. Thousands of

Chapter 12 — Expectancy

businesses would collapse. Life savings would be wiped out. People would have to look for alternatives if they were to survive."

Sara and Magda came into the room and our conversation, which I was really enjoying, ended.

"Why don't you get out of bed for a while, and come downstairs to the lounge room?" Sara proposed. They left me to shower and change before joining them downstairs.

"Did anything else happen on your way home?" Ivan asked, wanting to continue our previous conversation.

"I saw more trees and greenery than when I left," I recalled. "And I heard people talking about astrology as if it was a natural part of their daily conversation. Not the horoscopes you read in the newspaper each day, but with far more detail and understanding. They were making comments like, Jupiter is in the ninth house, and describing what that meant to them personally or to world events. They seemed so knowledgeable. It occurred to me this phenomenon was being studied in school and I was the only one who didn't understand it."

"I believe astrology will be studied more widely one day," Magda said, confirming my vision. "I've read recently scientists are finding a connection between our brain chemicals and the ocean tides and how they're both affected by the moon. Technology is so powerful now it is letting researchers make connections unheard of just a few years ago. When people open their minds to possibilities and scientists of every kind begin to work together, astrology will become part of the school curriculum. People will understand planetary influences affect their daily lives and can impact their life purpose."

"I've never studied astrology before," I said. "But I do know I'm an Aquarian. Now I would really like to know more."

"Give me the details of your birth; the date, time and year and I may be able to tell you a great deal more about your life," Ivan offered. Sara found a notepad and listed the birthdates for the family and then gave it to Ivan. He glanced at it and put the paper in his pocket.

"So, what happens next, Joshua?" Magda asked.

"I have to be clear about what I want my future to look like and then I have to make my intentions known to the universe. I know I want to offer workshops on every aspect of vision and to attract clients. I want to reach a wide audience and be a catalyst for their spiritual development."

"You can do all that," Magda assured me. "As long as you come back to this earthly plane and take your time. You can do it."

Magda and Ivan left our home shortly after and feeling inspired by our conversation, I went back to bed to think on it some more.

The next day I decided to start a journal and record all I had experienced on my trip to Queensland. I wanted to be sure I did not waste the lessons and the wisdom I

Chapter 12 *Expectancy*

had gained there. I also wanted to document it for my children, for them to read when they were older so they would understand. I found an exercise book and started to write down everything I did, saw and learned, including the large hot houses that produced food, the tree plantings, and the benefit and wisdom I discovered in astrology.

I wrote for hours and then reviewed all I had written. So much of what was important was still missing from my notes. I decided to communicate my thoughts from a place of learning.

'I learned,' I began, 'we must love unconditionally. When humanity recognises the most important phenomenon in the world is unconditional love, humankind will appreciate that is all we truly need. Then, we will become telepathically connected. Our lives will be expressed as an outpouring of beauty and compassion. The world will be a happier place. There will be peace throughout the world because we will find peace within ourselves. When we are aware of who we are, we become conscious of others. As our vibrations become more in tune with our Creator, new ways of healing will emerge. Drugs will be replaced by vibrational medicine that uses colour, sound and energy. We will be able to heal ourselves. We will know instinctively the needs of our bodies and we will have the means and resources to provide our bodies with the best and most healthy nutrients.'

Exhausted, I put my pen down and fell asleep. I dreamed I was the captain of a spaceship traveling the cosmos and exploring the stars. I returned to Earth to collect my twin brother whom I wanted to travel with me. I found him in a forest and transported him aboard the ship. He looked at the stars and the planets and then implored me to take him back to Earth. He said he didn't belong in the stars. When I awoke from the dream, I knew I also needed to ground myself on Earth and be in the present.

A few days later, I was at home alone when I received a phone call from Andrew.

"I'm calling for two reasons," he said. "Firstly, I wanted to thank you for what you said to me on the last day of the workshop. It's given me food for thought. So, thank you." After a short pause, he continued. "Secondly, I want to know how you are and to tell you, you must eat more bananas."

I was enjoying a banana at that very moment. "I'm eating one, right now," I told him. "I'm finding bananas ground me." We talked for a while longer and when we hung up, I recognised it was time for me to move on from Andrew. We had accomplished what we were meant to do for one another.

I still had the following week off work to recover from my trauma. My test results showed I had not been infected with any viruses from the mosquitoes and I was feeling much better. However, Sara was adamant I should stay home another week. When I went back to the accounting firm, I had a new attitude towards my work. I knew I was going to be ready to leave the job by the end of the year. But realistically and financially, I didn't see how that would be possible.

Chapter 12   Expectancy

Two weeks later, Jillian came over to our house and talked to Sara about her experiences and learnings at the Queensland workshop. She casually mentioned she had not seen me talking to any reporters at the airport. I was curious and went to look up the Townsville Gazette's phone number only to discover there was no such newspaper. There was no logical explanation for this. I had to assume I had met with angels, who had been sent to help me adjust as I returned to my life.

I was due for another test on my tumour. But I remembered how badly the magnets had affected me the last time I had an MRI, so I set an intention and asked my angels and guides to ensure the magnets created healing energy and did not drain the life force from me. I knew the magnets were simply a vibration, the same as any other healing energy, like colour.

The tests went well. I didn't feel any discomfort, so my goal was achieved.

"Are you feeling all right?" Sara asked me when I met her in the waiting room. "You look a little disorientated."

"I do feel a bit dazed," I told her. "The magnets seemed to affect me differently from the last time. I had set my intention for the procedure to be used for healing and it seems to have worked."

"Could you have received an over-dose of energy?" Sara asked.

"No one has ever mentioned that one can get too much energy!" I said, trying to understand.

That evening, as the effects of the MRI wore off, I was feeling drowsy.

Sara and I did our meditation and talked about needing more balance in our lives.

"I keep thinking about having more balance," Sara said. "During meditation, I contemplated about your description of the future and that we needed to live more in the present. We have to consider when and how it is appropriate to express our unconditional love, or people could misunderstand, and that would create more conflict." I agreed with Sara, recognising we needed time to integrate all we had learned from these new experiences.

Brian came by the house the next day, with a message for me. We talked about incorporating all my recent experiences in a way that would help me create the future I wanted.

"I can't see myself working in one healing modality at a time. For instance, I cannot just do Reiki; I would also incorporate the use of massage and other forms of energy work. I have found a way to integrate different therapies into my own form of healing and I'm confident they work better together than any alone." It felt positive being able to summarise my philosophy for the life I was creating.

"I think you're on the right track," Brian said, encouraging a meaningful conversation for both us. "We, as health practitioners, are going in the direction where, rather than being concerned about the modality

Chapter 12 — *Expectancy*

we use to heal, like Reiki for example, the healer will become the healing. You'll offer the *Joshua Method* and I'll use the *Brian Method*."

"That makes a lot of sense," I agreed. "I don't think there are two healers who do the same thing the same way. I have never received the same level of massage we provided to our clients."

When we had finished our discussion, Brian gave me a back massage and for the first time, in a long time, I felt myself returning to my new reality.

As soon as Brian had left, I prepared some tea for Sara to show her I was fine. Later in the day I took care of some tasks around the house. After dinner, Ivan and Magda arrived as we had planned to discuss astrology. Ivan took out the paper Sara had given him, with all our birth date details on it, along with his notes. "As you know astrology involves the forecasting of earthly and human events through the observation of the stars, the sun, the moon and the planets. We believe that these elements have a tremendous influence on our behavior and on earthly affairs.

"Most people associate their sun sign with astrology," Ivan told us. "However, the moon and the planets have a much greater influence. As you know, Joshua, your sun is in Aquarius which means you are unconventional and individualistic. Aquarians tend to be very creative and they like to build and develop ideas. But when you were born, your moon was in Capricorn, which influences your emotions and you tend to be very conservative in expressing your feelings. Mercury was in Pisces which means you are intuitive and open to new ways of seeing things, including spirituality."

Ivan continued to explain what the planetary influences meant for me and then he did the same for Sara and the children. Sara's influence was primarily the sun and Mercury being in Cancer, which meant she is very sensitive and keeps an orderly home.

"I can understand the meaning of Aquarian," I said. "But how do the planets fit in with astrology?"

"Each planet connects with a particular task," Ivan explained. "I'll go through each one for you. The sun is associated with our self-expression, our unique individuality, energy and enthusiasm. These are the characteristics astrologers like to focus on in newspapers and magazines. The sun is the more masculine element and the moon is more feminine and influences our emotional state, as well as our personality and moods." He stopped to see if we had any questions and then continued. "Mercury is linked to communication. It affects both our abilities to clearly express ourselves and to truly hear what another person is saying. It can also suggest times when you need to look more deeply into yourself for answers. Venus is the connection to love and social aspects of our lives. Mars, on the other hand, relates to work and physical energy. Jupiter is associated with career and completes its cycle every twelve years," Ivan explained.

I considered I had been an accountant for eleven years. "This is my twelfth year as an accountant." I added.

Chapter 12 — Expectancy

"In that case," Ivan smiled, "you had better be prepared to change careers next year."

"Please tell us about the other planets," Sara urged, very interested in the information Ivan was providing.

"Saturn helps you achieve your life's purpose, which may be different from what you had in mind. It teaches us lessons and prepares us for what we need, not necessarily what we want. This can be positive or negative, depending our perspective. But it is neither good nor bad. It just is. Uranus is the awakener. I suggest you have both had the influence of Uranus several years ago when it jolted you into opening your mind to new ideas and opportunities.

"Neptune does the opposite. It suspends your sense of reality and causes confusion and fear. You need to watch your ego does not counteract Neptune's influences, or you could lose hope. However, Neptune can make you more socially conscious and selfless. You carry out acts of kindness without expecting anything in return. Finally, Pluto fosters transformation and it's up to you to ensure the change is for the better and take advantage of the opportunities it provides."

"So much for free will with so many forces influencing us," Sara sighed.

Magda offered an answer. "The planets are there to influence us. We are free to respond however we want," she said. "We can go along with them or go against the current. If we move with the tide, our life can be so much easier."

"It's interesting to note, too," Ivan added, "that Cayce presented planetary effects as a reason for different phenomena happening. When asked about the weather, he often spoke of the influence of Jupiter and Uranus. He also saw astrology developing as mankind advanced."

"Talking about Cayce," I said, "I'd like to tell you about the dream I had last night."

"Go on," Ivan said, listening intently.

"It was a two-part dream. In the first part, I was at a fair the night before it was due to open. There were several empty stalls as the exhibitors had not set up yet. I was looking at a display of all sorts of power tools. In the second part of the dream, I walked down a corridor into a large room filled with tables of sandwiches and cakes. Edgar Cayce came up to me and said the food was free with entry into the fair. I told Edgar Cayce, I would be back and went home to get Sara."

Ivan interpreted the dream easily.

"The meaning of the dream is clear," he said. "The first part of the dream is telling you, you still have a lot to learn, like the tools of the trade. The second part of the dream provides some possible answers about what you should learn. Cayce represents someone who is pure of heart. Going home to collect Sara was telling you how important it is for you to share your life with Sara, especially the spiritual food Cayce has to offer."

I did want to share all my experiences with Sara, but I was beginning to realise how difficult it was for her to understand and appreciate what was happening to me. I was focusing on the future and she was possibly caught in the present.

On the weekend, I went by myself to Bendigo to deliver a vision workshop. This was the first time I was holding a workshop outside of Ballarat. I was planning more workshops and my dreams were being realised.

I was feeling strong and was able to guide the eight participants towards finding their vision. By the end of the weekend, several members of the group were experiencing new insights and understanding the importance of seeing with their hearts and not just with their eyes. As I drove home, I felt a tremendous sense of achievement having helped them take their first steps along their spiritual path. I was so much happier doing this work than dealing with the checks and balances of accounting.

In the evening, as I sat reviewing the events of the weekend, I had the idea of living in a community of like-minded people. As I meditated with Sara, I thought back to the time of Jesus and my life as an Essene. As I came out of the meditation, I found myself thinking of a prayer, *The Lord's Prayer*, and decided to write down what it meant to me.

'Father-Mother-God,' I wrote in my journal. 'We honour you. May your will be done to create Heaven on Earth. Help us to become co-creators. Help us to be less judgmental of others. Help us to live in peace and to find love. For true power lies there. Beyond time. Amen.'

One Vision

When I showed my prayer to Sara, she acknowledged there was a remarkable influence of the Essenes in my writing.

"Perhaps you should write down everything you've learned and share that with the world," she suggested with so much enthusiasm, I immediately replied.

"I agree with you. But I don't write well and I'm not sure I can do an adequate job."

"If you write from the heart," Sara assured me, "and with integrity, people will understand."

"I will think about it," I said. "Maybe one day I will write it all down. After all, they say, 'There's at least one book in each of us.'"

Life was fairly quiet until Easter. I had been invited to be an announcer at the spiritual festival I had first attended some three years earlier. It was the first time I was going to be on stage introducing speakers to large audiences and the prospect of doing it was thrilling. I had found my voice.

I presented James Christian, who was leading a choir, and following my introduction I joined them. After twenty minutes of groaning and sighing, we began to sing. It was an amazing experience. We sang in harmony and once again I had found my singing voice.

The next speaker I introduced was Rhiannon.

"Rhiannon," I declared, "is from Hawaii and is an expert on astrology. Please join her in Room One in five minutes." I was interested in her lecture, so I followed

Chapter 12 — Expectancy

her into the room. She believed astrology was the language of the future and her path was to teach the language.

During the day, I also met two people who taught the didgeridoo. Hearing the instrument played well, I felt a strong connection to it, so I attempted to play it. But, despite my best efforts, I could not get the proper sound from it.

"It takes time," my teacher told me. I recognised I did not have the gift to play this instrument and I was satisfied to listen to those who did.

When I arrived home, Sara reminded me to contact my doctor for the results of the recent tests on my tumour. I had been avoiding doing so because I no longer believed the doctors could tell me what needed to be done. Noticing my hesitation, Sara implored me to call. I learned from the doctor there was no change in the size of my tumour. I was disappointed it was still present in my life but decided to accept it for now and believe that anything could happen in the future.

My life at the accountancy firm was just as uncertain; my heart wanted nothing more than to run workshops, but my physical time was spent at the office. I still did not know how it would change, but I believed it would be soon. All I could do was to trust in God and to live in my own truth. I received a letter from Sharon in which she mentioned she had seen me talking to two people at the airport, which left me with more questions than answers.

One Vision

Sara and I decided to plan a family holiday because we were both aware I was finding it hard to stay balanced. She often had to tell me to slow down and be present. I would listen to her because I could see she had already achieved the balance for which I was aiming. Our love continued to grow because of her understanding.

I had another dream on Easter Sunday night. I dreamed I received a cross from a priest. I placed a symbol of a hand in the centre of the cross, which meant I was called to serve. On the left side of the cross, I put the symbol of a mouth to signify the need for open communication. When I was about to place a symbol on the right side, I was told to leave the wood blank for something was about to happen, but I did not yet know what.

About the Author

Barry Auchettl has overcome various physical and medical challenges in his life. He no longer needs to wear glasses and has survived a life threatening tumour on his pituitary gland, which inspired this fictional work.

In 1992, Barry was wearing multi-focal glasses, but he found wearing them was causing him headaches and considerable eyestrain. When he questioned the need for such strong lenses in his new glasses, he was told he would "get used to them". He decided instead to visit a behavioural optometrist. He also started to change his normal practice of putting on his glasses as soon as he awoke each morning. Later, Barry began to follow a program to improve his eye health which included eye exercises, meditation and self-healing.

After following this program for six months, Barry had the statement, 'Needs to wear glasses' removed from his driver's license. Then he started exploring other ways of 'seeing'. He has since completed courses in Reiki, Theta Healing, Kinesiology, and specific courses in vision and colour receptivity. His goal was to combine these healing modalities in order to help identify the needs of individual clients.

He has since completed a Master of Education degree, where he researched the effects of computers on eyesight. Barry is the author of "Eye Power", "The Scan Charts" and he is also the creator of "Conversations: an inspirational game."

Barry is committed to continuing his own personal development and helping others on their path to clarity. Barry has not only improved his physical eyesight, but also his 'in sight' and attitude towards others. Barry founded 'Eye Power'; a service devoted to helping people learn to see differently.

Barry is the principal of www.thevisionschool.org which focuses on initiating and launching visionaries who bring their own unique insight to the world. In 2020, Barry co-produced and launched with Nathan Oxenfeld, a program targeting children's eye health at www.computereyesprogram.com. He produced and featured in the documentary "Vision 2020: from eyesight to insight".

Although this novel is based on Barry's own experience, the names of people, the timing of events and the way some of the insights were revealed have been changed. Some characters are a compilation of different people Barry knew at that time.

Barry can be found at www.BarryAuchettl.com